The National Trust
for Scotland

CONTENTS

SEE PAGES 104-110 FOR QUICK REFERENCE
TO PROPERTY OPENING TIMES & CHARGES

**YOUR NEW GUIDE
NOW LASTS LONGER
2003 & 2004**

D0419784

The conservation charity that protects and promotes Scotland's
natural and cultural heritage for present and future generations
to enjoy. Charity no. SCO 07410

Enjoying Scotland's best   2
To help you get the most out of your visit   4

List of properties and descriptions, in areas
(for alphabetical index, see pages 111 & 112):

DUMFRIES & GALLOWAY   7
SCOTTISH BORDERS   11
EDINBURGH & THE LOTHIANS   15
FIFE   21
AYRSHIRE & ARRAN   25
GREATER GLASGOW & CLYDE VALLEY   31
ARGYLL, BUTE & LOCH LOMOND   38
CENTRAL SCOTLAND   43
PERTHSHIRE   49
ANGUS   53
ABERDEEN & GRAMPIAN   57
LOCHABER   67
WEST COAST ISLANDS   71
ROSS-SHIRE   76
INVERNESS, NAIRN, MORAY & THE BLACK ISLE   82
NORTHERN ISLANDS   86

Properties owned by the Trust and under guardianship
agreements or leased to others   88
Properties owned by the Trust but not open to the public   90
Members' Centres & Groups   91
The Road to the Isles   92
See how our gardens grow   94
Scotland's Gardens Scheme   94
A walk on the wild side   95
Ranger/naturalist service   96
Corporate Challenge   97
Conservation Volunteers   98
More ways to enjoy the countryside   99
Conservation through education   100
Little Houses Improvement Scheme   102
Scotland's Churches Scheme   102
Quick reference to property opening times & charges   104

Alphabetical index of properties   111
Map locating properties   inside back cover
Key to symbols & admission charge bands   inside back flap

A TASTE OF SCOTLAND'S QUALITY

The amazing breadth and quality of the Trust's portfolio offers something for everyone, not least the chance to enjoy fine food in the most amenable of surroundings. The Trust's restaurants, cafés and tearooms are furnished to complement their setting, and all share the aim of bringing the finest tastes of Scotland to your table. New this year is the refurbished and expanded restaurant at the Culzean Home Farm Visitor Centre, where the menu will appeal to all tastes. Sit and enjoy local delicacies, traditional Scottish dishes and treats for the children while taking in the spectacular views.

Your gaze may wander to the Isle of Arran, a magical place and a beautiful setting for Brodick Castle. The castle has both an excellent restaurant serving full meals or light snacks, and a new Courtyard Café, where you can enjoy good coffee, tea or light snacks in the relaxing ambience of our Plant Centre. At Threave Garden in the south-west, the newly refurbished restaurant offers tempting fare and tantalising views of the 60-acre garden beyond.

The Trust has always welcomed families and especially children – and this year there will be more on offer for everyone. When you have worked up an appetite enjoying our living history displays, state-of-the-art interpretation and unspoiled natural heritage, savour our unique approach to catering for all tastes. With lunch boxes and other treats, the whole family can enjoy the range and quality we offer.

 Our commitment to showcasing Scotland's quality is highlighted by our connection with Taste of Scotland, who this year are launching the national food grading scheme in association with VisitScotland. Look out for the Taste of Scotland symbol in this guide for an extra-special offering of warm hospitality and great home-produced food.

Shops and catering facilities are included in the property listings. Opening times as property, unless otherwise indicated. The seating capacity of catering facilities is given in brackets after the symbol.

CORPORATE HOSPITALITY, PRIVATE EVENTS & WEDDINGS

Throughout Scotland's history, Trust properties have played host to celebrations, banquets, historic meetings and gatherings. Continuing that tradition, Trust venues now offer perfect locations for romantic weddings, stylish corporate hospitality, elegant family celebrations and themed events. Within this guide, the symbol **F** denotes that a property is available to hire for functions of any kind. For further information on any of our venues, please telephone (0131) 243 9405, email us at functions@nts.org.uk or see our website, www.nts.org.uk/functions

SHOPS WITH SOMETHING FOR EVERYONE

You can be sure that when you visit our properties there is something in store for all the family, not least for the youngsters, who will now find an even larger range of fun gifts and souvenirs of their visit. At some of our historic properties our new range of toy swords and shields has proved to be very popular, especially during battle re-enactments at Fyvie or Bannockburn or a jousting display at Culzean.

On the subject of Culzean, please don't miss the opportunity of making the revamped Home Farm a regular place to shop. Here we offer a greatly expanded Home Farm Shop selling the very best of wholesome Scottish food and drink and, next door, new children's and gift shops make your shopping easier for all the family at a great location!

Remember, when you buy from us, you are directly helping us to protect Scotland's heritage.

visit www.nts.org.uk

TAKE A BIT OF OUR GARDENS HOME WITH YOU

We now have plant centres at many of our major garden properties, stocking top-quality plants mainly from our gardens, where they have been grown with minimal use of chemicals and peat. At Brodick Castle this is very much a feature.

There's something for everyone – from a simple packet of seeds for the children, to an exotic Japanese maple for the serious gardener. We carry a range of old-fashioned herbaceous plants alongside an ever-changing array of alpines and primulas. The famous blue poppy (*Meconopsis*) is as popular as ever, as is our collection of unusual plants.

Almost all our plant centres are suitable for visitors in wheelchairs. Opening times are the same as the shops, unless otherwise indicated. Every purchase helps to support the Trust's conservation work.

Brodick Castle Garden

Visits to properties

We welcome group visits, and would ask you, please, to book with your chosen property in advance, if your group is of 20 or more, including coach parties. Many property managers are pleased to arrange visits outwith normal opening hours. Please allow time for a relaxed and enjoyable visit: generally it will not be possible to tour a property after half-an-hour before closing time. To allow all visitors a pleasant visit, guided tours may be introduced at short notice to regulate visitor flow.

Special events

Many exciting events are held at our attractions, and our countryside properties have a full programme of guided walks: details are published in our *What's On* brochures, issued with our magazine in March, June and September, and also available from our properties or offices. Sometimes an extra charge may be made for events, whether held in or outwith property opening times. This applies also to Trust members, who are admitted free of charge during normal property opening times.

Public transport and cycling

In each entry for properties open to the public you will find information on public transport routes, where practicable, and on National Cycle Routes. For properties situated in major cities well served by bus and rail, we have not included public transport details. For general information on public transport throughout Scotland, tel Traveline Scotland (0870) 6082608; for rail information tel (08457) 484950. For more information on the National Cycle Network, tel Sustrans (0131) 624 7661; website www.sustrans.org.uk.

Visitors are advised that many buses stop only at the entrance gates to castles or large properties: from there, a walk through the grounds of up to a mile may be necessary to reach the property itself.

Public transport information is correct at time of going to press.

Disabled and less able visitors

The Trust welcomes disabled and less able visitors. Many of our major properties make special provisions and numerous other properties are accessible. We regret that at some smaller properties, the historic nature of the building makes access difficult. At most properties, disabled drivers may park and disabled passengers may alight right outside. While disabled visitors are charged the usual admission price, any necessary companion is admitted free. A free brochure describing both the facilities and limitations for disabled and less able visitors is available from Trust Offices, listed on page 6. It is also available in large print, Braille and audio-tape editions: to order, contact Trust head office. To ensure a comfortable visit, and to find out detailed information about access, we recommend contacting the property in advance of your arrival.

Photography and filming

The Trust welcomes photography for personal purposes in the grounds of all its properties, but for reasons of conservation and security and to avoid inconvenience to other visitors, we regret that we cannot allow photography or filming inside our historic buildings. Those wishing colour transparencies for lecture or other purposes may obtain these from our Photo Librarian at Trust head office; tel (0131) 243 9315.

Help conserve the treasures in our care

We encourage visitors to experience our properties to the full – and simply ask that you observe a few sensible precautions when you visit us. Please do not wear sharp heels, which can damage our wooden floors and carpets. We welcome young children to our historic houses, where they may be carried in the arms or in front slings, but the risk of accidental injury to visitors or damage to fragile furnishings or ornaments means that we cannot, unfortunately, admit prams, push-chairs or baby back carriers.

Please do not use metal detectors on Trust properties. Smoking is not allowed inside our built properties.

Dogs

At many of our properties special 'dog walks' are signposted and shaded areas are reserved for parking cars in which dogs are to be left. Please ask for details at the property you wish to visit. You are welcome to exercise your dog in open areas, car parks and other designated areas, but please keep them on a lead, and don't allow them to foul picnic areas or footpaths.

We welcome guide-dogs for the blind and deaf throughout our properties, but regret that other dogs are not permitted inside buildings, walled and enclosed gardens or in the immediate area beside buildings that are open to the public.

Free entry to our own and other National Trusts' properties

Members of the National Trust for Scotland are entitled to free admission to the properties owned and administered by the Trust and which are normally open to the public. Please don't forget to bring your current membership card with you, since we regret we can't admit you without it! Membership cards are not transferable.

Members are also granted free admission by the National Trust to properties belonging to and fully administered by them.

The National Trust for Scotland also grants free admission to our properties to members of other National Trusts from around the world. Our members are granted free or concessionary admission by these National Trusts to properties in Australia, Bahamas, Barbados, Bermuda, Canada, Cayman Islands, Eire, Fiji, Guernsey, India, Isle of Man, Jamaica, Jersey, Malaysia, Malta, New Zealand, Virgin Islands and Zimbabwe. For details contact Membership Services at Trust head office.

The National Trust

The National Trust is a separate organisation covering England, Wales and Northern Ireland whose address is 36 Queen Anne's Gate, London SW1H 9AS; tel (020) 7222 9251; email enquiries@thenationaltrust.org.uk, website www.nationaltrust.org.uk.

Details of National Trust properties in England, Wales and Northern Ireland are published in the National Trust Handbook, which is available at our own shops or by post from:

Antique Collectors' Club, Sandy Lane, Old Martlesham, Woodbridge, Suffolk, IP12 4SD; tel (01394) 389977, fax (01394) 389999, email abs@antique-acc.com.

Visitor attraction quality assurance

VisitScotland has introduced a quality assurance scheme for visitor attractions. Awards provide an assurance that the standards of facilities and services provided at an attraction have been independently verified by one of their grading officers. Look out for the distinctive plaques on your visits.

Volunteers

Enormous help is given to the Trust by over 2,500 volunteers. Working in a voluntary capacity can suit many people who wish to extend their interests, meet new people or develop their levels of experience for future careers. Openings arise at properties all over Scotland for volunteers to undertake a variety of tasks, from clerical and administrative work to guiding or helping out in gardens, restaurants or retail outlets. If you would like to find out more about working as a volunteer, please contact the Trust at head office.

More information?

If we haven't answered your question about visiting us, or on any other topic concerning the Trust, please contact our head office or one of our four regional offices, and we'll be pleased to help you.

visit www.nts.org.uk

Head Office

Wemyss House, 28 Charlotte Square,
Edinburgh EH2 4ET (see p 16).
Tel: (0131) 243 9300 Fax: (0131) 243 9301
Website: www.nts.org.uk
Chief Executive: Robin Pellew, PhD

North-East Region

The Stables, Castle Fraser, Sauchen,
Inverurie AB51 7LD
Tel: (01330) 833225 Fax: (01330) 833666
Director: David Sharland

Highlands and Islands Region

Balnain House, 40 Huntly Street,
Inverness IV3 5HR
Tel: (01463) 232034 Fax: (01463) 732620
Director: Alex Lindsay

South Region

Northgate House, 32 Northgate,
Peebles EH45 8RS
Tel: (01721) 722502 Fax: (01721) 726000
Director: David McAllister

West Region

Greenbank House, Flenders Road,
Clarkston, Glasgow G76 8RB
Tel: (0141) 616 2266 Fax: (0141) 616 0550
Director: Michael Hunter

London

19 Cockspur Street, London SW1Y 5BL
Tel: (020) 7321 5765 Fax: (020) 7389 0758
London Representative: Malcolm Innes

North America

Suite 576, One Boston Place, Boston, MA 02108
Tel: (617) 619 3631
Email: nationaltrustforscotland@gurland.com
Counsel: Johanna Gurland

The National Trust for Scotland gratefully acknowledges the financial support for conservation projects throughout Scotland provided by our principal funding partners: the European Union European Regional Development Fund and the European Agricultural Guidance and Guarantee Fund; the Heritage Lottery Fund; the National Heritage Memorial Fund; Historic Scotland; and Scottish Natural Heritage.

   HISTORIC SCOTLAND

Receipt of financial assistance from local authorities, local enterprise companies and other companies, trusts and individuals is also gratefully acknowledged. Details are provided in the Trust's Annual Review and Accounts, which are available on request.

Key to Symbols

Please refer to the inside back flap of this guide for the key to symbols and price band information. Open out for easy reference.

For public transport information **Tel Traveline Scotland (0870) 6082608**

The National Trust
for Scotland

DUMFRIES & GALLOWAY

Threave

This south-west corner of Scotland offers unexpectedly dramatic contrasts, its uplands, lochs, forests and coastline vying with those of the Highlands in beauty. A mild climate and unspoilt environment favour unusual wildlife and a variety of plants, nowhere more evident than at the Trust's Threave Garden, where the fascinating Maxwelton Collection of local domestic and agricultural bygones is now on display for the first time at the Visitor Centre.

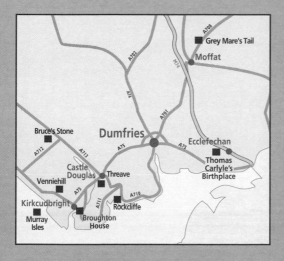

Broughton House   Broughton Garden   Bruce's Stone   Thomas Carlyle's Birthplace

A Band F: see back flap

L Explanatory text in French and German

♿ Access difficult

➔ Off A711/A755. On National Cycle Route 7. Bus: McEwans (Nos 500/X75, 501) from Dumfries and Castle Douglas, stop in Kirkcudbright; tel (08457) 090510

BROUGHTON HOUSE & GARDEN

12 High Street, Kirkcudbright, Dumfries & Galloway DG6 4JX.
Tel/fax (01557) 330437; email broughtonhouse@nts.org.uk

18th-century town house of the Murrays of Broughton and Cally, which was bought in 1901 by E A Hornel, the renowned artist and member of 'The Glasgow Boys'. Between 1901 and 1933 he added an art gallery and a studio overlooking the fascinating garden with Japanese influences, which leads down to the estuary of the Dee. The House is expected to be closed for extensive restoration during the 2003 season. The garden will remain open, though access may be limited at certain times. Please check with property.

The E A Hornel Trustees transferred ownership of the house to The National Trust for Scotland in 1997.

OPEN	House may be closed during 2003 and for part of the 2004 season for major conservation works. In 2003, garden open 1 Feb to 31 Mar and 1 to 20 Oct, Mon-Fri 11-4; 1 Apr to 30 Sep, Mon-Sat 11-5, Sun 1-5. Some restrictions may apply at certain times: for details of these and 2004 opening times/admission charges for house and garden, please check with property.

Enquiries to South Regional Office; tel Peebles (01721) 722502

➔ By A712, 3m W of New Galloway

BRUCE'S STONE

Moss Raploch, Dumfries & Galloway.

It is said that King Robert the Bruce rested against this stone after using guerrilla tactics to defeat an English army here in 1307.

Given by the Earl of Mar in 1932.

OPEN	All year, daily.

A Band E: see back flap

♿ Access difficult

🚩📖 ✳

➔ Off M74, on A74, in Ecclefechan, 5¹/₂m SE of Lockerbie, 6m NW of Gretna Green. On National Cycle Route 74. Bus: White Star and Stagecoach, from Lockerbie to Ecclefechan; tel (08457) 090510 Rail: Lockerbie station, 5¹/₂m; tel (08457) 484950

THOMAS CARLYLE'S BIRTHPLACE

The Arched House, Ecclefechan, Lockerbie,
Dumfries & Galloway DG11 3DG. Tel (01576) 300666.

The Arched House, in which Thomas Carlyle was born on 4 December 1795, was built by his father and uncle (both master masons) in 1791. Carlyle was a great writer and historian and one of the most powerful influences on 19th-century British thought. The interior of the house is furnished to reflect domestic life at Carlyle's time and also on show is a notable collection of portraits and his belongings.

Given in 1936 by the Trustees of Carlyle's House Memorial Fund.

OPEN	1 May to 30 Sep, Thu-Mon 1-5.

Grey Mare's Tail

Murray Isles

<Rockcliffe

GREY MARE'S TAIL NATURE RESERVE

Moffat Valley, Dumfries & Galloway.

A magnificent upland property of 870 ha (2,150 a), unfolding from the waterfall that cascades into the Moffat valley up steep slopes to the post-glacial Loch Skene and its corries beyond. The summit of White Coombe (821 m) is the highest point. A landscape shaped by human activity since the Iron Age, it lies on a historic communications route and has strong connections with the Covenanters who sought sanctuary here in the 17th century. The property is botanically outstanding and contains the richest collection of rare upland plants in southern Scotland: it is now a Special Area of Conservation. A Visitor Centre offers CCTV views of a peregrine falcon nest site and a panoramic view of hillside features. Programme of guided walks throughout summer.

This property of 870 ha (2,151 a), extending to Loch Skeen and White Coomb, was purchased in 1962 by the Trust's Mountainous Country Fund formed by Percy Unna. A further 52 ha (128 a) at Dob's Linn were purchased in 1972.

OPEN	All year, daily.

Ranger/naturalist (based at Threave) tel (01556) 502575

♿ Visitor Centre accessible, but surrounding terrain difficult

🚶 Note: There have been several fatal accidents at this property. It is extremely dangerous to leave the paths. Please heed warning notices. Please ensure you wear boots and are appropriately dressed for walking in the hills.

R

P Band H: see back flap

➔ On A708, 10m NE of Moffat

MURRAY ISLES Dumfries & Galloway.

Two small uninhabited islands in the Islands of Fleet, Wigtown Bay, off Carrick Point. The islands are host to a colony of cormorants and are significant as a site for breeding gulls.

Gifted to the Trust in 1991 by Mrs Murray Usher of Cally OBE.

OPEN	All year, daily.

Enquiries to South Regional Office; tel (01721) 722502

➔ Near Gatehouse of Fleet, off A75. Near National Cycle Route 7. Accessible only by boat. Please do not visit during bird breeding season, May-July

ROCKCLIFFE Dumfries & Galloway.

48 ha (119 a) of coastline within a National Scenic Area, with a network of paths including the Jubilee footpath from Kippford to Rockcliffe. A range of habitats support a wide variety of flora and fauna. Programme of guided walks in summer.

Muckle Lands and Jubilee Path given by Hilda G Longworth of Greywalls, Rockcliffe, in 1965.

Mote of Mark, 8-ha (20-a) site of an ancient hill-fort, and **Rough Island,** 8-ha (20-a) bird sanctuary. Owing to the sensitivity of ground-nesting birds, please do not visit the island during May and June.

Given by Messrs John and James McLellan in 1937 in memory of their brother, Col William McLellan, CBE, of Orchard Knowes. Auchenvhin (two cottages and 7 acres) bequeathed to the Trust in 1969 with an endowment by Major J I A McDiarmid. In October 1971 Mrs M E McLellan of Glenluffin, Rockcliffe, presented 3.84 ha (9.5 a) of coastline near the Merse, Rockcliffe. In September 1990 Mrs M Anderson of Waterfoot, Rockcliffe, presented .4 ha (1 a) of coastline near the Merse.

OPEN	All year, daily.

For enquiries tel (01556) 502575

♿ Toilet at Rockcliffe

🚶 R P

➔ Off A710, 7m S of Dalbeattie

Key to Symbols

Please refer to the inside back flap of this guide for the key to symbols and price band information. Open out for easy reference.

Threave>

NEW FEATURE

A House & garden, Band A; garden only, Band C: see back flap

L Explanatory text in French, German, Italian, Spanish

Most of garden and house, Visitor Centre, restaurant, shop. Toilet. Wheelchairs and electric battery cars available. Reserved places in car park

Induction loop in Visitor Centre

Dog walk

Open as Visitor Centre

(80, plus 40 on terrace). 'Taste of Scotland'. Open as Visitor Centre

Off A75, 1m W of Castle Douglas. On National Cycle Route 7.
Bus: McEwan's (No 501) from Dumfries to Castle Douglas; tel (08457) 090510

THREAVE

Castle Douglas, Dumfries & Galloway, DG7 1RX.
Tel (01556) 502575; fax (01556) 502683; email threave@nts.org.uk
Ranger/naturalist: tel (01556) 502575.

Threave Garden is delightful in all seasons. At 26 ha (64 a), it is best known for its spectacular springtime daffodils (nearly 200 varieties), but herbaceous beds are colourful in summer and trees and heather garden are striking in autumn. The Victorian house is home to the Trust's School of Practical Gardening. The principal rooms in **Threave House** opened to the public for the first time in 2002 and have attracted great interest. The interiors have been restored to their appearance in the 1930s, and from the house visitors can enjoy impressive vistas of the Galloway countryside. Guided walks. Maxwelton Collection of local bygones in the Visitor Centre on show for the first time in 2003. Plant Centre.

Threave Estate is a wildfowl refuge and is designated a Special Protection Area for its breeding waders and wintering wildfowl. The important wetlands are designated an Area of Special Scientific Interest. Threave provides a good example of integrated management of the land, taking account of agriculture, forestry and nature conservation. Marked walks include a 2.5-km estate trail through this variety of landscapes, and hides provide good cover to observe bird activity. A Countryside Centre in the old stables highlights nature conservation, forestry and agriculture at Threave.

The house and estate, 492 ha (1,215 a), were given in 1948 by Major A F Gordon, DSO, MC, of Threave, with a generous endowment. A further adjoining 113 ha (279 a) were purchased in 1950 and 1959.

OPEN	
	Estate and garden, all year, daily 9.30-sunset.
	Walled garden and glasshouses, all year, daily 9.30-5.
	Visitor Centre, Countryside Centre and exhibition, 1 Feb to 31 Mar and 1 Nov to 23 Dec, daily 10-4; 1 Apr to 31 Oct, daily 9.30-5.30.
	House, 1 Mar to 31 Oct, Wed, Thu, Fri and Sun, 11-4 (guided tours only, maximum 10 people, two per hour, admission by timed ticket).

Enquiries to South Regional Office; tel (01721) 722502

Car park for disabled visitors only. Picnic site accessible

Off A75. 1m from National Cycle Route 7

VENNIEHILL

Gatehouse of Fleet, Dumfries & Galloway.

1.4 ha (3.5 a) of wildflower-rich grassland with a hilltop viewpoint, at the west end of the main street, managed to encourage diversity of flora and associated invertebrates. The hilltop is partially surrounded by a low earth work, perhaps the defence structure of an old fort or early settlement.

Gifted to the Trust in 1981 by Mrs Murray Usher of Cally OBE.

OPEN	
	All year.

The National Trust
for Scotland

SCOTTISH BORDERS

Robert Smail's Printing Works

A land of contrasts — a dramatic, rugged coastline, site of the spectacular St Abb's Head nature reserve where, this year, a remote camera link allows visitors to watch nesting birds. Inland, green hills cradle ruined abbeys and historic towns like Melrose, home to the Trust's tranquil Priorwood Garden. Here, uniquely, plants are grown specifically for their beauty when dried, and events and workshops explore this age-old craft.

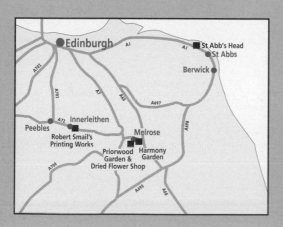

Edinburgh

A1

St Abb's Head
St Abbs

Berwick

A697

A702

A703

A7

A68

A697

A698

A72

Innerleithen

Peebles

Robert Smail's
Printing Works

Melrose

Priorwood
Garden &
Dried Flower Shop

Harmony
Garden

A708

A698

A68

**For more information contact
The National Trust for Scotland
SOUTH REGION**
Northgate House
32 Northgate
Peebles EH45 8RS
Tel (01721) 722502

visit www.nts.org.uk

<Harmony Garden   Priorwood Dried Flower Shop   Priorwood Garden

Enquiries to
South Regional Office:
tel (01721) 722502

 Band F: see back flap

Much of garden accessible.
Parking at entrance

➡ In Melrose, opposite the
Abbey. On National Cycle
Route 1. Bus: First Edinburgh
from Edinburgh and Peebles
to Melrose;
tel (0131) 663 9233

HARMONY GARDEN
St Mary's Road, Melrose, Borders TD6 9LJ.

A delightfully tranquil walled garden comprising lawns, herbaceous and mixed borders, vegetable and fruit areas, and a rich display of spring bulbs. The garden is set around an early 19th-century house (not open to the public), built by Melrose joiner Robert Waugh, who named it 'Harmony' after the Jamaican pimento plantation where he had made his fortune. Harmony Garden has excellent views of Melrose Abbey and the Eildon Hills and is situated near Priorwood Garden (see separate entry).

Bequeathed in 1996 by Mrs Christian Pitman.

OPEN	Good Friday to Easter Monday and 1 Jun to 30 Sep, Mon-Sat 10-5, Sun 1-5.

Band E; see back flap

Ramp to shops and garden.
Parking usually available
at entrance

➡ Off A6091, in Melrose,
adjacent to Abbey. On
National Cycle Route 1.
Bus: First Edinburgh from
Edinburgh and Peebles to
Melrose; tel (0131) 663 9233

PRIORWOOD GARDEN & DRIED FLOWER SHOP
Melrose, Borders, TD6 9PX.
Tel (01896) 822493, fax (01896) 823181;
email priorwooddriedflowers@nts.org.uk
Shop: Tel (01896) 822965.

A specialist garden where most of the plants grown are suitable for drying. The colourful and imaginative selection ensures variety for the dried flower arrangements made here. Visitors can enjoy a stroll through the orchard which includes historic varieties of apples that are organically grown. Enjoy the different blossoms in spring, a picnic here in the summer, and catch a glimpse of the impressive ruins of Melrose Abbey which overlook the garden. Priorwood Garden is a short walk from Harmony Garden (see separate entry). For information on day courses throughout the year, please contact the property.

Purchased in 1974.

OPEN	Good Friday to Easter Monday, 1 May to 30 Jun and 1 Sep to 24 Dec, Mon-Sat 12-5, Sun 1-5; 1 Jul to 31 Aug, Mon-Sat 10-5, Sun 1-5	Trust shop, 6 Jan to 31 Mar, Mon-Sat 12-4; 1 Apr to 24 Dec, Mon-Sat 10-5, Sun 1-5.

Key to Symbols
Please refer to the inside
back flap of this guide for
the key to symbols and price
band information. Open out
for easy reference.

visit www.nts.org.uk

St Abb's Head

<Robert Smail's Printing Works

ROBERT SMAIL'S PRINTING WORKS

7/9 High Street, Innerleithen, Borders, EH44 6HA.
Tel (01896) 830206; email smails@nts.org.uk

Step back in time at this completely restored printing works and see how printing was done at the beginning of the 20th century. The buildings contain an office, paper store with reconstructed water-wheel, composing and press rooms. Visitors can watch the printer at work and try typesetting by hand. Historic items and photographs give a fascinating insight into this small Borders town.

Purchased from Cowan Smail in 1986.

OPEN	Good Friday to Easter Monday and 1 Jun to 30 Sep, Thu-Mon 12-5 (Sun 1-5)

A Band D: see back flap

& Shop, office and machine room. Disabled visitors may alight at front door

⬆ ▶

➡ 30m S of Edinburgh. On National Cycle Route 1. Bus: First Edinburgh from Edinburgh or Peebles; tel (0131) 663 9233

ST ABB'S HEAD
NATIONAL NATURE RESERVE

Scotland's National Nature Reserves

Ranger's Cottage, Northfield, St Abbs, Eyemouth, Borders, TD14 5QF.
Tel (018907) 71443, fax (018907) 71606.

Formed by an extinct volcano, the Head is the best known landmark along the magnificent Berwickshire coast. Home to thousands of nesting seabirds in summer, the Head also has a wealth of other wildlife and fine views along the coast. In recognition of its importance to both wildlife and people, the Head was declared a National Nature Reserve in 1983. The offshore waters lie within a Special Area of Conservation and form part of Scotland's only Voluntary Marine Nature Reserve. New remote camera link to Nature Reserve Centre allows visitors to observe seabirds during nesting season (recorded footage out of season). Exhibition, toilets.
Purchased in 1980.

Lumsdaine Farm coastal strip. 68 ha (168 a) of cliff and foreshore donated to the Trust by the Pearl Assurance Company Ltd in 1984. Part of the same Grade 1 Site of Special Scientific Interest as St Abb's Head.

Blackpotts grazing block. 50 ha (123 a) purchased in 1994 to alleviate grazing pressure on the clifftop during summer.

A Nature Reserve Centre. Band H: see back flap

& Toilet. Free parking. Nature Reserve Centre accessible though some wheelchair users may need assistance. Remote camera link to nesting birds. Access by car to lighthouse

🐕 Dogs must be kept on leash

🍽 (not NTS)

📖 R

P Band I. Please use car park beside Nature Reserve Centre at Northfield Farm steading: no vehicles on road to lighthouse except those carrying disabled, elderly or infirm visitors

➡ Off A1107, 2m N of Coldingham

OPEN	Nature Reserve and toilets, all year, daily.	Nature Reserve Centre, 1 Apr to 31 Oct, daily 10-5 (groups by appointment only).

A NEW BEGINNING

MORE NEW TRAINS THAN EVER BEFORE, WITH REVOLUTIONARY FEATURES INCLUDING AN ON-BOARD SHOP,
AT-SEAT AUDIO AND POWER POINTS. THIS IS ONLY THE START. MORE NEW TRAINS WILL SOON BE
ARRIVING ON OUR SCOTTISH ROUTES. WE PROMISED A NEW BEGINNING AND NOW WE'RE DELIVERING.

VISIT VIRGIN.COM/TRAINS OR CALL 08457 222 333

The National Trust for Scotland

EDINBURGH & THE LOTHIANS

One of Europe's most beautiful cities, Scotland's capital combines history with a thriving cosmopolitan atmosphere. The Trust owns properties typical of the medieval Old Town and the elegant New Town, as well as fascinating gardens and houses within easy reach of Edinburgh. Newhailes, a 'Sleeping Beauty' town villa in its intriguing policies, is one of the area's newest attractions.

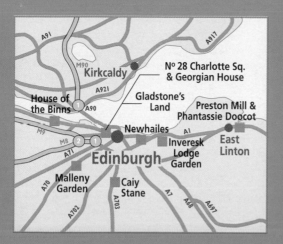

Newhailes

**For more information contact
The National Trust for Scotland
SOUTH REGION**
Northgate House
32 Northgate
Peebles EH45 8RS
Tel (01721) 722502

visit www.nts.org.uk

<No 28 Charlotte Square>

Enquiries to
South Regional Office;
tel (01721) 722502

Easy access on pavement

→ Off B701, Oxgangs Road, 2m from National Cycle Route 75

A Free

L Explanatory text in French, German, Italian, Japanese and Spanish

Wheelchair access through entrance in Hope Street Lane, where disabled visitors may park, though narrow street is often congested. All public areas and toilets accessible with assistance

P No parking on site, but public spaces on west side of Charlotte Square

E

→ In Edinburgh city centre, 2 mins from west end of Princes Street. On National Cycle Routes 1 and 75

CAIY STANE Caiystane View, Edinburgh.

This impressive 2.7-m (9-ft) tall prehistoric cup-marked stone, also known as General Kay's Monument, or the Kel Stone, traditionally marks the site of an ancient battle, perhaps between Picts and Romans.
Given by Mrs Johnston Gee in 1936.

OPEN	All year, daily.

Nº28 CHARLOTTE SQUARE

Edinburgh EH2 4ET. Tel (0131) 243 9300, fax (0131) 243 9301.
Restaurant reservations, private dining and functions (0131) 243 9339; email catering@nts.org.uk

Charlotte Square, in Edinburgh's renowned New Town, is considered by many as the finest Georgian square in Britain. It was the last commission of Robert Adam (1728-92), one of the world's most influential architects. The square's light, spacious town houses attracted Scottish landowners and professional people, who could afford to move out of the crowded tenements of the Old Town, and the south side's first feus were sold in 1796.

During the 20th century the houses on the south side were used increasingly as offices by legal and financial companies, many of whom had moved out by the early 1990s. In 1996 the Trust bought Nos 26-31, with the vision of initiating a renaissance of the square. The houses are now the head office of the Trust, with The Drawing Room Gallery, Gift Shop, Coffee House and Restaurant open to visitors. On display is a collection of 20th-century Scottish paintings, including works by the Scottish Colourists, which has been donated to the Trust. It is complemented by a loan collection of fine Regency furniture and objets d'art. The Drawing Room Gallery also acts as an information centre about the Trust and its work. There is a wide range of exciting goods in the shop, and visitors can enjoy morning coffee, light lunch or afternoon tea in style in the Coffee House. The 'Taste of Scotland' restaurant offers a lunch menu with fresh seasonal produce in a relaxed atmosphere.
Nos 26-31 Charlotte Square were purchased by the Trust in April 1996.

OPEN	Drawing Room Gallery, Mon-Fri 11-3.
All year.	Shop, 6 Jan to 24 Dec, Mon-Sat 10-5.
	Coffee House and Restaurant, open at 9.30.

For public transport information
**Tel Traveline Scotland
(0870) 6082608**

<The Georgian House   Gladstone's Land>

THE GEORGIAN HOUSE

7 Charlotte Square, Edinburgh EH2 4DR. Tel/fax (0131) 226 3318 or tel (0131) 225 2160; email thegeorgianhouse@nts.org.uk

The Georgian House is part of Robert Adam's masterpiece of urban design, Charlotte Square. It dates from 1796, when those who could afford it began to escape from the cramped, squalid conditions of Edinburgh's Old Town to settle in the fashionable New Town. The house's beautiful china, shining silver, exquisite paintings and furniture all reflect the domestic surroundings and social conditions of the times. Video programme. New touchscreen programme featuring a virtual tour of the house.

Nos 5, 6 and 7 Charlotte Square were conveyed to the Trust through National Land Fund procedures in 1966. The lower floors of 7 Charlotte Square were opened in 1975.

OPEN	House and shop, 1 to 31 Mar and 1 Nov to 24 Dec, daily 11-3; 1 Apr to 31 Oct, daily 10-5.

A Band C: see back flap

L Explanatory text in Chinese, Danish, Dutch, French, German, Italian, Japanese, Portuguese, Russian, Spanish, Swedish

♿ Limited (6 steps to ground floor). Parking outside house

👁 Braille guidebook

🔊 Induction loop; sub-titled video

🛍 📖 F

→ In Charlotte Square, 2 mins from west end of Princes Street; 10 mins from Tourist Information Centre. On National Cycle Routes 1 and 75

GLADSTONE'S LAND

477B Lawnmarket, Edinburgh EH1 2NT.
Tel (0131) 226 5856; fax (0131) 226 4851.

Gladstone's Land is a typical example of a 17th-century tenement building of the overcrowded Old Town which grew up along the ridge between Edinburgh Castle and the Palace of Holyroodhouse – the Royal Mile. The building is the most important example of 17th-century high-tenement housing to survive in Edinburgh. Its site and the extent of its accommodation mark its prestige in terms of mercantile dignity. The cramped conditions of the Old Town determined the width of the lot on which the house was built, which meant that extension was only possible in depth or height. Completed in 1620, the six-storey building contains remarkable original painted ceilings. The reconstructed shop booth displays replicas of 17th-century goods and the first floor has been refurbished as a typical Edinburgh home of the period.

Purchased in 1934.

OPEN	1 Apr to 31 Oct, Mon-Sat 10-5, Sun 2-5

A Band D: see back flap

L Explanatory text in Dutch, French, German, Italian, Japanese, Norwegian, Spanish

♿ Ground floor; gift shop. Four steep steps from road to pavement. No parking outside

👁 Braille guidebook

🛍 📖 ✹

→ In the Lawnmarket (part of the Royal Mile), 5 mins' walk from Tourist Information Centre in Princes Street via the Mound. 1m from National Cycle Routes 1 and 75

House of the Binns> *Inveresk Lodge Garden*

A Band C: see back flap
Members of the Royal Scots
Dragoon Guards, successors
of 'The Greys', in uniform,
are admitted free

L Explanatory text in Chinese,
Dutch, French, German,
Japanese, Polish, Russian,
Spanish

♿ Lower floor only: photograph
album showing interiors of
upper floors. Parking at main
door by arrangement. Toilet

Braille information sheets

🐕 No dogs allowed in parkland

🎋 Off A904, 15m W of
Edinburgh.
Rail: Linlithgow Station 3m;
tel (08457) 484950

HOUSE OF THE BINNS

Linlithgow, West Lothian, EH49 7NA. Tel (01506) 834255;
email houseofthebinns@nts.org.uk. Ranger Service: tel (0131) 665 1546.

The House of the Binns is the historic home of the Dalyells, among them
General Tam Dalyell who raised the Royal Scots Greys here in 1681.
Parts of the present house date from the time of General Tam's father
(1612-30). It reflects the early 17th-century transition in Scottish
architecture from fortified stronghold to more spacious mansion.
Important moulded plaster ceilings in four of the main rooms were
added in 1630. The furniture dates mostly from the late 18th and early
19th centuries. There is also an excellent run of family portraits and an
interesting collection of china. Woodland walk to panoramic viewpoint
over Firth of Forth, with beautiful snowdrops and daffodils in spring.

*Given by the late Eleanor Dalyell of The Binns in 1944, with pictures, plenishings and an endowment.
87 ha (215 a).*

OPEN	House,1 Jun to 30 Sep, daily except Fri, 2-5. Pre-booked tours in May by arrangement with the Property Manager	Parkland, 1 Apr to 31 Oct, daily 10-7, 1 Nov to 31 Mar, daily 10-4.

Enquiries to
South Regional Office;
tel (01721) 722502.

A Band F: see back flap

♿ Access to conservatory and
some of garden. Toilet.
Parking at entrance

🐕 No dogs in garden, please

P Cars may only be parked by
garden wall

🎋 A6124, S of Musselburgh,
6m E of Edinburgh.
1m from National Cycle
Route 1. Bus: Lothian
Region Transport from
Edinburgh city centre,
tel (0131) 555 6363

INVERESK LODGE GARDEN

24 Inveresk Village, Musselburgh, East Lothian, EH21 7TE.

This inviting terraced garden in the historic village of Inveresk entices
visitors with its colourful herbaceous beds, a variety of attractive shrubs
and a collection of old roses selected by Graham Stuart Thomas. Plants
and methods are demonstrated here that can be used in your own
garden. The fine Edwardian conservatory has an aviary, tree ferns and
hardy exotics. In the informal area, many of the plants hold the Royal
Horticultural Society's Award of Garden Merit. The sunny hillside garden
provides the setting for the 17th-century Inveresk Lodge (not open to
the public) and offers distant views of the Pentland Hills.

Presented to the Trust in 1959 by Helen E. Brunton.

OPEN	All year, daily 10-6 or dusk if earlier.

visit www.nts.org.uk

Newhailes>

Malleny Garden

MALLENY GARDEN

Balerno, Edinburgh, EH14 7AF. Tel (0131) 449 2283.

This 1.2-ha (3-a) walled garden has a delightful collection of old-fashioned roses and fine herbaceous borders, and also houses the National Bonsai Collection for Scotland. A particular feature of the garden is the four 400-year-old clipped yew trees, but there is also extensive woodland for a peaceful stroll surrounded by wildlife. The house was built for Sir James Murray of Kilbaberton around 1635. Its two Georgian reception rooms, added in 1823, are opened by the Friends of Malleny on occasion during the summer.

Presented to the Trust with an endowment by the late Mrs Gore-Browne Henderson in 1968.

OPEN	Garden, all year, daily 10-6 or dusk if earlier.

NEWHAILES

Newhailes Road, Musselburgh, East Lothian, EH21 6RY.
Tel (0131) 653 5599 (advance booking advisable, especially at peak times).

Newhailes is a fine late 17th-century house with impressive 18th-century additions and interiors, set in a fascinating 18th-century designed landscape. The house was built by the distinguished Scottish architect James Smith in 1686, and bought in the early 1700s by Sir David Dalrymple, of the Scots legal and political dynasty, who were responsible for significant improvements and additions to the house, and for one of the most important rococo interiors in Scotland. The most remarkable addition was the library, which played host to many famous figures of the Scottish Enlightenment and was reportedly described by Dr Johnson as 'the most learned room in Europe'. The house contains a fine collection of paintings, including portraits by Sir John de Medina and Allan Ramsay.

Much of the original decoration and furnishing has survived intact, though worn. The Trust is working to conserve the house in such a way as to leave it as 'untouched' by modern hands as possible, retaining the mellowness of its interiors rather than attempting the recreation of an immaculate dwelling as first built.

(continued over the page)

A Band F: see back flap

L Rose garden guide in French, German and Italian

Garden. Disabled visitors may alight and enter at small gate by Malleny House

P E

→ Off Lanark Road (A70). 1m from National Cycle Route 75. Bus: Lothian Region Transport (No 44) from Edinburgh city centre; tel (0131) 555 6363, or First Edinburgh (Nos 44/66); tel (0131) 663 9233

A House: Band B. Policies and parking only Band H: see back flap

L Explanatory text in French and German

Principal floor of house and Visitor Centre. All-ability path through the policies

Dedicated dog area

(not NTS)

R P

→ Off Newhailes Road (A6095). 1m from National Cycle Route 1. Bus: Lothian Region Transport (No 40) from Edinburgh city centre; tel (0131) 555 6363. Rail: Musselburgh station 15 mins' walk

Newhailes>

The important 18th-century designed landscape is a source of intriguing discovery, revealing beneath the overgrowth a raised walkway, grotto, woodland walks and a wealth of local wildlife. Ongoing research, including archaeological work, examination of the diaries of Christian Dalrymple and other historical documents, will help inform the Trust's perspectives for restoration of the landscape. Visitors will be able to witness this gradual process rather than seeing freshly restored gardens.

House and policies donated by the Trustees of Sir C M Dalrymple. Contents acquired in 1997.

OPEN	Policies, all year, daily 10-6.	House and Visitor Centre, 1 Apr to 30 Sep, Thu-Mon 12-5; 1 to 31 Oct, Sat/Sun 12-5.
Visits to the house by 1¼-hour guided tour only: booking advised.		

A Band D: see back flap

L Explanatory text in Dutch, French, German, Italian, Japanese, Spanish

♿ Ground floor, shop, grounds. Toilet. Disabled visitors may alight at mill

🏠 ⛽ 🚶 ▣ 🅿

➡ Off A1, in East Linton, 23m E of Edinburgh. Bus: First Edinburgh from Edinburgh to East Linton; tel (0131) 663 9233

PRESTON MILL & PHANTASSIE DOOCOT
East Linton, East Lothian, EH40 3DS. Tel (01620) 860426.

There has been a mill on this site since the 16th century, and the present stone buildings date from the 18th century. The conical roofed kiln and attractive red pantiled buildings make Preston Mill a popular haunt for photographers and artists, while the nearby millpond with resident ducks and geese provides the finishing touches to an idyllic countryside spot. The water-wheel and the grain milling machinery it powers are relatively modern and the mill was still used commercially until 1959. Visitors can see and hear the mechanisms in action and find out about the working life of a miller. Exhibition on milling and display on history of Preston Mill and the people who lived and worked here.

Given by the Trustees of John Gray in 1950.

Phantassie Doocot, a short walk away, once held 500 birds.

Given in 1962 by William Hamilton of Phantassie Farm.

OPEN	1 Apr to 30 Sep, Thu-Mon 12-5 (Sun 1-5).

Preston Mill

Preston Mill

FIFE

The ancient 'Kingdom' of Fife was prominent in the history of medieval Scotland. Falkland Palace powerfully evokes the days of the Stuart monarchs, for whom this was a favourite country retreat. The beautiful Kellie Castle now has a fascinating new exhibition on the sculptor Hew Lorimer, who lived and worked here.

The Royal Burgh of Culross

Perth

Dundee

A913

A90

A92

A9

A94

A90

Balmerino Abbey

Hill of Tarvit Mansionhouse & Garden

A91

St. Andrews

A92

A915

A91

Falkland Palace & Garden

Kellie Castle & Garden

A917

A91

A911

A92

A915

A823

A92

Kirkcaldy

A921

Royal Burgh of Culross

A985

Edinburgh

A1

<The Royal Burgh of Culross

Balmerino Abbey

Enquiries to NTS South Regional Office; tel (01721) 722502

A Band F: see back flap

♿ Grounds accessible in dry weather. Parking adjacent to abbey

→ Off A914, 5m W of Tay Road Bridge; 10m NW of St Andrews. On National Cycle Route 1

A Band C: see back flap

L Guidebook in French and German. Video in French and German for groups. Explanatory text in Dutch, French, German, Hebrew, Italian, Japanese, Spanish

♿ Most of exhibition and ground floor of Palace. Tearoom. Toilet. Disabled visitors may alight at Town House, Palace and Study

Braille guidebook. Audio tour

Induction loop in Town House and Bessie Bar Hall; subtitled video

(45) In Bessie Bar Hall: opens at 11 when Palace opens at 12.30

F P

→ Off A985, 12m W of Forth Road Bridge, 4m E of Kincardine Bridge, 6m W of Dunfermline, 15m W of Edinburgh city centre. 3m from National Cycle Route 76. Bus: Stagecoach Fife Buses or First Edinburgh Central, Dunfermline-Stirling route; tel (01383) 621249 or (01324) 613777

BALMERINO ABBEY
Balmerino, Fife.

Ruins of a Cistercian monastery, founded in 1229. Visitors may not enter the buildings, which are undergoing stabilisation work, but can view them from the grounds, which contain an ancient Spanish chestnut tree, one of the oldest in the country.

Given to the Trust in 1936 by the Earl of Dundee.

OPEN	All year.

THE ROYAL BURGH OF CULROSS
Culross, Fife KY12 8JH. Tel (01383) 880359; fax (01383) 882675.

This small royal burgh on the north shore of the Forth provides a striking introduction to Scottish domestic life in the 16th and 17th centuries. Culross was then a thriving community, with mining, iron working and salt panning, and a flourishing trade with other Forth ports and the Low Countries. Culross was also the birthplace of St Mungo or Kentigern, patron saint of Glasgow and founder of its cathedral. Culross Palace was built between 1597 and 1611 and features original interiors with painted woodwork, 17th- and 18th-century furniture and decorative items, and a fine collection of Staffordshire and Scottish pottery.

A model 17th-century garden has been built to the rear of the Palace. It contains a variety of unusual vegetables, herbs and perennials, all available in 1600.

The Town House and The Study are both open to the public, while The Ark, Bishop Leighton's House, The Nunnery and other restored houses may be viewed from the outside only. Visitor reception and exhibition/DVD on the royal burgh of Culross in Town House: shown to groups in Bessie Bar Hall. Audio tour of Palace.

The burgh's present appearance is the result of continuing restoration by the Trust over some 50 years, aimed at achieving modern living standards while preserving characteristic architecture. The Palace was bought by the Trust in 1932 and placed under the guardianship of the then Office of Works (now Historic Scotland). In 1991 the Trust assumed full management responsibility for the Palace, which was reopened to the public in 1994 following a major restoration programme. The Trust also owns the Town House, presented by the royal burgh in 1975, and The Study. The ruined St Mungo's Chapel, built in 1503 by Archbishop Blackadder on the traditional site of the saint's birth, was presented to the Trust by the Earl of Elgin in 1947.

OPEN	Palace, Study, Town House, shop and tearoom, Good Friday to 30 Sep, daily 12-5. Shop also open 1 Oct to 31 Dec, Sat/Sun 12-4. Garden, all year, daily 10-6 or sunset if earlier.

Plant Centre at Falkland Palace

Living history at Falkland Palace

Mary, Queen of Scots

FALKLAND PALACE, GARDEN & OLD BURGH

Falkland, Cupar, Fife KY15 7BU.
Tel (01337) 857397; fax (01337) 857980; shop (01337) 857918.

The Royal Palace of Falkland was the country residence of Stuart kings and queens when they hunted deer and wild boar in the Fife forest. Mary, Queen of Scots spent some of the happiest days of her tragic life here, 'playing the country girl in the woods and parks'. The Palace was built between 1501 and 1541 by James IV and James V, replacing earlier castle and palace buildings dating from the 12th century, traces of which can still be seen in the grounds. The roofed South Range contains the Chapel Royal, and the East Range the King's Bedchamber and the Queen's Room, both restored by the Trust. The Keeper's Apartments in the Gatehouse are now also on display. The palace contains fine portraits of the Stuart monarchs and two sets of 17th-century tapestry hangings.

The garden, designed and built by Percy Cane between 1947 and 1952, contains three herbaceous borders enclosing a wide lawn with many varieties of shrubs and trees. Here also is the original Royal Tennis Court – the oldest in Britain still in use – built in 1539. There is also a small herb garden border featuring quotations from John Gerard's book *Herball* (1597). Exhibitions at Royal Tennis Court and at Town Hall.

In 1952, Major Michael Crichton Stuart, MC, MA, Hereditary Constable, Captain and Keeper of Falkland Palace, appointed the Trust as Deputy Keeper and provided an endowment fund for future upkeep. The palace still belongs to Her Majesty the Queen but is maintained and managed by the Trust. In 1970 the first Conservation Area in Scotland was established in Falkland, 4.5 ha (11 a) embracing the Palace with its gardens and orchard, and the adjoining oldest part of the royal burgh. This area is particularly rich in 'little houses', of which some 20 owe their restoration to the late Keeper or the Trust. Falkland Town Hall was bought by the Trust in 1986.

A Palace and garden, Band B; garden only, Band D see back flap. Scots Guards and members of the Scots Guards Association (wearing the association's badge) admitted free

L Guidebook in French and German. Explanatory text in Dutch, French, German, Italian, Japanese, Spanish, Swedish

♿ Garden wheelchair available. Ramp into garden. Access to Palace very difficult. Disabled visitors may alight at Palace

❀ Scented garden

👓 🛍 🌱 🍴 🎨 **F P E** ✳

➡ A912, 10m from M90/junction 8, 11m N of Kirkcaldy. On National Cycle Route 1. Bus: Stagecoach Fife stops in High Street (100 metres); tel (01592) 610686

OPEN	1 Mar to 31 Oct, Mon-Sat 10-6, Sun 1-5.	Shop also open 1 Nov to 24 Dec, daily 10-4; 3 Jan to 28/29 Feb, hours vary: please contact property for details.

Falkland Palace

Hill of Tarvit Mansionhouse>   Kellie Castle

A House, Band C; garden and grounds only, Band H: see back flap

L Explanatory text in Dutch, French, German, Italian, Japanese, Spanish

& Front-door ramp to ground-floor rooms. Some paths in garden accessible. Toilets. Wheelchair available. Parking at house

Short dog walk in woodland

(44)

F P
E

→ Off A916, 2m S of Cupar. 1m from National Cycle Route 1. Bus: Stagecoach Fife to village of Ceres, 1m; tel (01334) 474238. Rail: Cupar station 2m; tel (08457) 484950

HILL OF TARVIT MANSIONHOUSE & GARDEN
Cupar, Fife KY15 5PB. Tel/fax (01334) 653127; email hilloftarvit@nts.org.uk

The present house was remodelled in 1906 by Sir Robert Lorimer for Mr F B Sharp to form a suitable setting for his notable collection which includes French, Chippendale-style and vernacular furniture, Dutch paintings and pictures by Raeburn and Ramsay, Flemish tapestries and Chinese porcelain and bronzes. The interior is very much in the Edwardian fashion. The formal gardens to the south were also designed by Lorimer. Restored Edwardian laundry. Path to hilltop panoramic indicator. See also Scotstarvit Tower (page 89).

Bequeathed in 1949 by Miss E C Sharp with 503 ha (1,243 a) of gardens, forest and farmland as endowment. The present holding is 198 ha (489 a). Until 1977 the upper floor was used as a convalescent home by the Marie Curie Foundation.

OPEN	1 Apr to 30 Sep, daily 1-5; 1 to 31 Oct, Sat/Sun 1-5.	Tearoom, same dates, but opens at 12.	Garden and grounds, all year, daily 9.30-sunset.

A Castle, Band C; garden, grounds and parking only, Band H: see back flap

L Explanatory text in French, German, Italian, Japanese, Spanish, Swedish

& Garden and ground floor of castle; tearoom. Wheelchair available. Parking at castle

Video induction loop

(18) **F**
P E

→ On B9171, 3m NNW of Pittenweem

KELLIE CASTLE & GARDEN
Pittenweem, Fife, KY10 2RF. Tel (01333) 720271; fax (01333) 720326.

Kellie Castle is a very fine example of the domestic architecture of Lowland Scotland. The oldest part is believed to date from 1360, but the building in its present form is mainly 16th- and early 17th-century and was completed about 1606. Sympathetically restored by the Lorimer family around 1878, it contains magnificent plaster ceilings, painted panelling and furniture designed by Sir Robert Lorimer. New exhibition commemorating Hew Lorimer's life and work. Audio tour of garden.

The layout of the organic walled garden is 17th-century with late Victorian additions and contains a fine collection of old-fashioned roses, fruit trees and herbaceous plants. Display in summer-house on history of walled garden.

The castle, garden (restored by Mr and Mrs Hew Lorimer and the Trust) and 6.5 ha (16 a) were purchased in 1970; the main contents were given into the care of the Trust by the Secretary of State for Scotland. In 1998 the Trust purchased the Lorimer family artifacts.

OPEN	Castle, Good Friday to Easter Monday and 1 Jun to 30 Sep, daily 1-5.	Tearoom, same dates but opens at 12.	Garden and grounds, all year, daily 9.30-sunset.

The National Trust for Scotland

AYRSHIRE & ARRAN

Culzean Castle

An accessible escape from the bustle of Scotland's central belt, the multi-faceted landscape of Arran is surprisingly unspoilt. Ayrshire's rolling hills, long sandy beaches and famous golf courses combine with the fascinating museums and monuments of Burns Country for wonderful days out. The Trust's top visitor attraction, the romantic Culzean Castle, now offers even more exciting facilities.

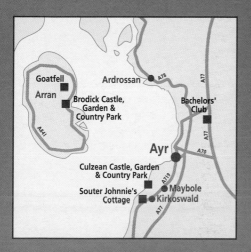

Goatfell
Arran
Ardrossan A78
A77
Brodick Castle, Garden & Country Park
Bachelors' Club
A841
Ayr
A77
A70
Culzean Castle, Garden & Country Park
A719
Souter Johnnie's Cottage
Maybole
Kirkoswald
A77

For more information contact
The National Trust for Scotland
WEST REGION
Greenbank House
Flenders Road, Clarkston
Glasgow G76 8RB
Tel (0141) 616 2266

visit www.nts.org.uk

Bachelors' Club   Brodick Country Park>

A Band E: see back flap

& Access limited. Parking outside house

→ In Tarbolton, off A77 S of Kilmarnock and off A76 at Mauchline, 7½m NE of Ayr. Bus: ½-hourly from Ayr; tel (0870) 6082608

BACHELORS' CLUB
Sandgate Street, Tarbolton, South Ayrshire, KA5 5RB.
Tel (01292) 541940 during opening times.

In this 17th-century thatched house, Robert Burns and friends formed a debating club in 1780. Burns attended dancing lessons, and was initiated into Freemasonry here, in 1781. Period furnishings.

Purchased in 1938.

OPEN	1 Apr to 30 Sep, Fri-Tue 1-5. Morning visits available for pre-booked groups.

A Castle and garden, Band B; garden and country park only, 1 Apr to 31 Oct, Band D; 1 Nov to 31 Mar, Band G: see back flap

L Guidebook in French and German. Explanatory text in Dutch, French, German, Italian, Japanese, Norwegian, Spanish, Swedish

& Reception Centre, shop and restaurant. Toilets in castle, Reception Centre and Countryside Centre. Parking for disabled beside castle. Electric bus from Reception Centre to castle. Self-drive electric battery car for grounds bookable in advance at castle. Wilma's Walk nature trail is suitable for disabled visitors. Access difficult to principal floor of castle and parts of Gardens & Country Park where paths are steep. Wheelchair available. Parking at castle

BRODICK CASTLE, GARDEN & COUNTRY PARK
Isle of Arran, KA27 8HY. Tel (01770) 302202; fax (01770) 302312; email brodickcastle@nts.org.uk.
Countryside walks and events: tel (01770) 302462.

The site of this ancient seat of the Dukes of Hamilton was a fortress even in Viking times. The 13th-century fortified tower was developed in the 16th century and extended by Cromwell in the 17th century. Lady Mary Louise, 6th Duchess of Montrose, lived here until 1957. Some furniture dates from the 17th century, with superb paintings, porcelain and silver collected by the Hamiltons and by William Beckford, whose daughter was married to the 10th Duke of Hamilton. There is also a collection of sporting pictures and trophies.

The woodland garden, begun in 1923 by the Duchess, is now home to an internationally acclaimed rhododendron collection. The walled garden dating from 1710 has been restored as an Edwardian garden. Find out about the garden's fascinating history and plant collections in a new audio tour. The Country Park has waymarked trails, woodlands, waterfalls, gorges, wildlife ponds, a nature room and wildlife garden. Restored ice-house, adventure playground.

In 1958 the castle and 'associated chattels' were accepted in lieu of estate duty by the Commissioners of Inland Revenue and in turn, accepted by the Trust at the request of the Treasury. The gardens and policies form a Country Park managed by the Trust on behalf of the Joint Committee representing North Ayrshire Council and The National Trust for Scotland.

OPEN	1 Apr to 31 Oct, daily 11-4.30 (closes 3.30 in Oct).
	Reception Centre, shop and walled garden, same dates but open at 10. Restaurant, same dates but closes at 5. Reception Centre also open 1 Nov to 21 Dec, Fri/Sat/Sun 10-3.30.
	Country Park, all year, daily 9.30-sunset.

Brodick Garden

Goatfell

RO3

RO20

- Braille information sheets
- Dog walk
- (75) 'Taste of Scotland'
- On National Cycle Route 73. Ferry from Ardrossan to Brodick (55 mins) and connecting bus to Reception Centre (2m). Ferry between Claonaig (Kintyre) and Lochranza (north Arran), frequent in summer, limited in winter. Ferry details, tel Caledonian MacBrayne, (0870) 565000; bus details, tel (0870) 6082608. All-inclusive travel and admission ticket from Strathclyde Passenger Transport rail stations; tel (0870) 6082608

- Access for walkers from Brodick Country Park and from Cladach on A841 Brodick-Lochranza. Near National Cycle Route 73

GOATFELL

Isle of Arran. Tel (01770) 302462.

The open, wild and rugged Goatfell is reminiscent of landscapes more typically found in the Scottish Highlands, providing opportunities for walking and mountaineering in a dramatic and challenging upland landscape yet easily accessible. It is nationally and internationally important for its landscape and geological features as well as for the extensive moorland and associated bird species. Goatfell, at 874 m (2,866 ft), is the highest peak on the Isle of Arran and offers spectacular views of the island and, on a clear day, across to Ben Lomond, Jura and the coast of Ireland.

Goatfell and neighbouring mountainous country were gifted in 1958 by Lady Jean Fforde, daughter of Mary, Duchess of Montrose.

| OPEN | All year, daily. |

For public transport information
Tel Traveline Scotland (0870) 6082608

The Vinery

Culzean Castle

NEW VISITOR FACILITIES

A Combined ticket (Castle & Country Park), Band A. Country Park, Band C: see back flap. Social inclusion concession scheme.

L Guidebook in French and German. Explanatory text in Dutch, French, German, Italian, Japanese, Spanish

Castle and Visitor Centre exhibition (via lifts); shops; restaurant and Coffee Shop; walled garden and Fountain Court garden; hide at Swan Pond; some paths in Country Park. Toilets at Visitor Centre, Castle, Croy Shore and Swan Pond Court. Wheelchairs and self-drive electric battery cars available (should be booked in advance). Some paths uneven in places. Parking at castle

Braille guidebooks. Tactile models. Tapping rails on some paths

Induction loop in auditorium

In Country Park

Details page 99

CULZEAN CASTLE & COUNTRY PARK
Maybole, South Ayrshire, KA19 8LE.
Functions, events and Eisenhower Apartment,
tel (01655) 884455; fax (01655) 884503; email culzean@nts.org.uk
website www.culzeancastle.net
Group/school bookings, ranger service,
Country Park information, tel (01655) 884400, fax (01655) 884522.

The Castle
Robert Adam converted a rather ordinary fortified tower house into this elegant bachelor residence for David Kennedy, 10th Earl of Cassillis, between 1777 and 1792. He also built a 'Roman' viaduct and Ruined Arch to add drama to this Italianate castle in its spectacular clifftop setting. Both the exterior stonework and the interior of the castle have been restored by the Trust. It contains a fine collection of paintings and furniture, and a display of weapons in the Armoury. The Circular Saloon has a superb panoramic view over the Firth of Clyde and the beautiful Oval Staircase is Robert Adam's final masterpiece of interior design.

In 1945 the top floor was given to General Eisenhower as a token of Scotland's recognition of his role during World War II. His apartment is now run as a small country house hotel, and an Eisenhower Exhibition in the castle tells something of Ike the man and his visits to Culzean. The Georgian Kitchen gives a glimpse of life below stairs 200 years ago. Educational programmes and tours are available. Through the Clocktower Courtyard, a coach-house and stables have been converted into the Castle Shop and Old Stables Coffee House.

The Country Park
Scotland's first country park, created in 1969 and consisting of 228 ha (563 a) contains a wealth of natural and historical interest. Miles of woodland walks take the visitor to the Deer Park, along the Cliff Walk or to the many restored estate buildings, such as the Ruined Arch and

Fountain Court Garden

The Picture Room

The Oval Staircase

<Culzean Country Park

Viaduct, beautiful Camellia House and unique Pagoda. Garden areas include the terraced Fountain Court and the Walled Garden with its redesigned pleasure garden and impressive reconstructed Victorian Vinery. The exciting adventure playground introduces children to the wildlife of the park and makes the Swan Pond a perfect spot for a family picnic.

The Visitor Centre, formerly the Home Farm, is the focus for the main visitor facilities. These include the Home Farm Restaurant, the Home Farm Shop, the Country Park Shop and Plant Centre. The new auditorium and exhibition at the Visitor Centre explain the history of Culzean and the Trust's conservation work, and there are smaller interpretive centres at the Gas House, Ice House and Swan Pond. Three miles of coastline provide panoramic views across the Firth of Clyde and improved facilities have been provided at Croy Shore – 1½ miles of beach – accessed from the A719. The ranger service provides an extensive environmental education service and interpretive programme.

Culzean was given to the Trust in 1945 by the 5th Marquess of Ailsa and the Kennedy family. The Country Park is managed by the Trust on behalf of a joint committee representing South Ayrshire Council and The National Trust for Scotland. Restored Dolphin House and new Bunkhouse leased to South Ayrshire Council as an Outdoor Education Centre.

OPEN	Castle, 1 Apr to 31 Oct, daily 10.30-5 (last entry 4).
	Visitor Centre, 1 Apr to 31 Oct, daily 9-5.30; 1 Nov to 31 Mar, Sat/Sun 11-4.
	Other visitor facilities, 1 Apr to 31 Oct, daily 10.30-5.30.
	Country Park, all year, daily 9.30-sunset.

SOUTER JOHNNIE'S COTTAGE

Main Road, Kirkoswald, South Ayrshire, KA19 8HY.
Tel (01655) 760603.

The home of John Davidson, village souter (shoemaker), who was the original Souter Johnnie of Robert Burns' *Tam o' Shanter*. Life-sized stone figures of the Souter, Tam, the innkeeper and his wife are in the restored ale-house in the cottage garden. The thatched cottage, recently refurbished, contains period furniture, Burns relics and a reconstructed souter's workshop.

The Trust took over the cottage in 1932 from the local committee that had restored it.

OPEN	1 Apr to 30 Sep, Fri-Tue 11.30-5.

Castle Shop, Home Farm Shop (with Scottish Food Hall) and Country Park Shop

Visitor Centre Restaurant (200) ('Taste of Scotland') and Old Stables Coffee Shop (36), plus snack-bars in Country Park.

P Band H: see back flap

12m S of Ayr, on A719, 4m W of Maybole, off A77. 4m from National Cycle Route 7. Bus passes main entrance; tel (0870) 6082608

Souter Johnnie's Cottage

Band E: see back flap

L Explanatory text in Dutch, French, German, Italian

Accessible throughout (not toilet)

P Local authority car park at S end of village

On A77, in Kirkoswald, 4m SW of Maybole. 4m from National Cycle Route 7. Bus: tel (0870) 6082608

GREATER GLASGOW & CLYDE VALLEY

There is much to explore in the exuberant architectural heritage of this vibrant city and its environs. The Trust's houses and gardens, whether humble or grand, typify the finest designs of their period. Browse and buy at the *Glasgow Style* exhibition in Hutchesons' Hall; or enjoy lunch in Pollok House's Edwardian Kitchen Restaurant, consistently awarded accolades by 'Taste of Scotland'.

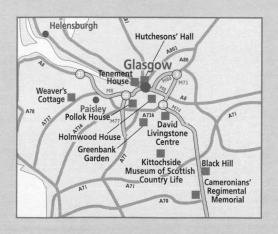

Pollok House

**For more information contact
The National Trust for Scotland
WEST REGION**
Greenbank House
Flenders Road, Clarkston
Glasgow G76 8RB
Tel (0141) 616 2266

visit www.nts.org.uk

Cameronians' Regimental Memorial   Greenbank Garden>

→ Off B7018 between
Kirkfieldbank and
Lesmahagow,
3m W of Lanark

BLACK HILL
South Lanarkshire.

A rich archaeological complex and spectacular viewpoint over the Clyde valley. Site of a Bronze-Age burial cairn, an Iron-Age hill-fort adjoined by a settlement enclosure, and field dykes which may date to the prehistoric and medieval periods. The site was designated a Scheduled Ancient Monument in 1969.

Given in 1936 by Messrs Robert Howie and Sons. 2 ha (5 a).

OPEN	All year, daily.

→ Off A70, 2m W of M74,
junction 12. 1m from
National Cycle Route 74.
Bus: hourly service
Lanark-Douglas;
tel (0870) 6082608

CAMERONIANS' REGIMENTAL MEMORIAL
Douglas, South Lanarkshire.

Statue of the Earl of Angus who was the first Colonel of the Cameronian Regiment which was raised at Douglas in 1689. The statue is situated at north edge of village.

Given to the Trust with an endowment in 1991 by the Cameronian Trust.

OPEN	All year, daily.

A Band D: see back flap
& Garden, shop, tearoom.
Toilets. Special garden and
greenhouse. Wheelchairs
available. Some woodland
paths uneven. Access to
house difficult. Parking at
reception building. Advice for
disabled gardeners
🐕 No dogs in garden, please
🏠 🛍(40) Open as shop
🛏🍴🌳📖 F E
→ Flenders Road off Mearns
Road, Clarkston. Off M77
and A726, follow signs for
East Kilbride to Clarkston
Toll. 6m S of Glasgow city
centre. 4m from National
Cycle Routes 7 and 75.
Bus: from city centre
along Mearns Road;
tel (0141) 333 3708

GREENBANK GARDEN
Flenders Road, Clarkston, Glasgow G76 8RB. Tel (0141) 616 5126.

A one-hectare (2.5-a) walled garden and 6 ha (15 a) of policies surround the elegant Georgian house, built in 1764 for a Glasgow merchant. The attractive garden indicates how wide a range of ornamental plants, annuals, perennials, shrubs and trees can be grown in the area and is especially relevant to owners of small gardens. Demonstrations.

The Trust was enabled to accept the gift of house and land by Mr and Mrs William Blyth in 1976 through the success of a public appeal for an endowment.

OPEN	Garden, all year, daily 9.30-sunset.	Shop and tearoom, 1 Nov to 31 Mar, Sat/Sun 2-4; 1 Apr to 31 Oct, daily 11-5.	House, 1 Apr to 31 Oct, every Sun 2-4.

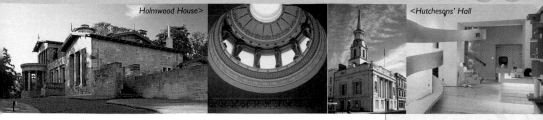

Holmwood House>

<Hutchesons' Hall

HOLMWOOD HOUSE

61-63 Netherlee Road, Cathcart, Glasgow G44 3YG.
Tel/fax (0141) 637 2129; email holmwood@nts.org.uk

Holmwood has been described as the finest domestic design by
Alexander 'Greek' Thomson. It was built in 1857-8 for James Couper,
who with his brother Robert owned Millholm Paper Mills on the banks
of the River Cart, below the house. The architectural style of the house
is a picturesque adaptation of classical Greek. Many rooms are richly
ornamented in wood, plaster and marble. Thanks to investigation by
Historic Scotland, Thomson's original rich decoration, based on themes
from the classical world, is beginning to emerge. Much of the original
stencilled decoration has been found, and visitors may follow the
progress of continuing conservation work. The small kitchen garden is
planted with a range of Victorian herbs, fruit and vegetables and the
house is surrounded by wildflower-rich woodland. Audio tour, CD-ROM.
The house may now be booked for corporate use.

The Trust acquired the property from the Sisters of Our Lady of the Missions in 1994.

OPEN	1 Apr to 31 Oct, daily 12-5. Morning visits available for pre-booked groups.

HUTCHESONS' HALL

158 Ingram Street, Glasgow G1 1EJ. Tel (0141) 552 8391;
fax (0141) 552 7031; email hutchesonshall@nts.org.uk

One of the most elegant buildings in Glasgow's city centre, Hutchesons'
Hall was built in 1802-5 to a design by David Hamilton. It incorporates
on its frontage the statues, from an earlier building of 1641, of the
founders of Hutchesons' Hospital, George and Thomas Hutcheson.
A major reconstruction in 1876 by John Baird heightened the Hall and
provided an impressive staircase. The interior is hung with portraits of
Glasgow worthies. A permanent multi-media exhibition, *Glasgow Style*,
includes film and a gallery selling work by young Glasgow designers.

The acquisition of the building in 1982 was made possible by use of the Trust's Golden Jubilee Appeal Fund.

OPEN	Gallery, shop and function hall, 20 Jan to 24 Dec, Mon-Sat 10-5.	Hall on view subject to functions in progress.

A Band D: see back flap

L Audio tour in French and German

& House and grounds. Toilet. Wheelchair lift to first floor

◉◉

Selection of 'Greek' Thomson-related goods and books of architectural interest

Refreshments in kitchen court

P

→ Netherlee Road, off Clarkston Road, B767, Cathcart. 2m from National Cycle Routes 7 and 75. Bus: frequent service from city centre along Clarkston Road; rail: frequent trains to Cathcart station (1m); tel (0870) 6082608

A Band F (function hall and A/V programme): see back flap

& Gallery and shop (up one small step). Toilet. Parking on street outside

F E

→ Ingram Street, near SE corner of George Square. 1m from National Cycle Routes 7 and 75

<Kittochside, the Museum of Scottish Country Life

A Adult £3, concession £1.50; 18 and under, NTS members and Friends of NMS free

& Exhibition building, café, shop and toilets. Transport to farm. Access difficult to upper floor of farmhouse, parts of farm steading and some uneven paths. Parking at main door

→ On northern edge of East Kilbride, between A726 and A749. From M74, turn off at junction 5; from M77, turn off at junction 3. Bus: First Glasgow (No 31) from city centre stops opposite museum entrance. Rail: frequent service to East Kilbride station (3m)

KITTOCHSIDE, THE MUSEUM OF SCOTTISH COUNTRY LIFE

Stewartfield Way, East Kilbride, Glasgow, G76 9HR.
Tel (01355) 224181

The Museum of Scottish Country Life has been created as a partnership between the Trust and National Museums of Scotland whereby the Trust owns the land and buildings, and National Museums has brought the National Country Life Collection to Kittochside and is responsible for the management and operation of the Museum.

The project has been made possible by the gift of Wester Kittochside Farm to the Trust in 1992 by Mrs M S C Reid. The gift, which included the contents of the farmhouse and steading, reflects the history and ownership of the land by ten generations of the Reid family since the 16th century, and illustrates many of the changes in Scottish farming practices over 300 years. The farm will be worked using the techniques and equipment of the 1950s, to demonstrate this late phase of the Agricultural Revolution. Additional land was purchased from South Lanarkshire Council in 1997 for a new purpose-built exhibition building and to provide land for special events to illustrate the life of the countryside.

OPEN	All year, daily 10-5 (closed 25/26 Dec and 1/2 Jan).

Kittochside, the Museum of Scottish Country Life

<David Livingstone Centre>

DAVID LIVINGSTONE CENTRE

165 Station Road, Blantyre, South Lanarkshire, G72 9BT.
Tel (01698) 823140.

Scotland's most famous explorer and missionary was born here in Shuttlerow in 1813. Today the 18th-century tenement commemorates David Livingstone's life and work. His childhood home – consisting of just one room – remains much as it would have been in Livingstone's day and gives the visitor an insight into the living conditions endured by industrial workers in the 19th century. The rest of the museum tells the story of Livingstone's explorations in Africa, with many of his personal belongings and travel aids, including diaries, navigational equipment and even the famous red shirt he was wearing when he met the journalist H M Stanley. Exhibition: new sculpture of Livingstone and the Lion.

The birthplace of Livingstone was rescued by public subscription in 1929. The management of the Centre was transferred to the Trust in April 1999 by the Governors of the Scottish National Memorial to David Livingstone Trust. A partnership was formed between the Trust, the Governors, South Lanarkshire Council and Scottish Enterprise Lanarkshire to raise funds for the operation and development of the Centre and to enable the Trust to assume ownership.

OPEN	1 Apr to 24 Dec, Mon-Sat 10-5, Sun 12.30-5.

SCULPTURE
NEW FOR 2003

A Band D: see back flap

L Explanatory text in Afrikaans, French, German, Italian, Spanish and Swahili

Access to all parts of Centre. Toilet

Large print interpretation

Sensory tours for visitors with learning difficulties (book in advance)

Just off M74, Junction 5, via A725 and A724; in Blantyre. 1m from National Cycle Route 75. Bus: from Buchanan Bus Station, Glasgow; rail: frequent service from Glasgow Central to Blantyre station (500 metres); tel (0870) 6082608

Pollok House>

Edwardian Kitchen Restaurant, Pollok House

A 1 Apr to 31 Oct, Band C: see back flap: free, 1 Nov to 31 Mar

L Explanatory text in French, German, Italian and Spanish

♿ House, shop, restaurant and servants' quarters. Wheelchair lift to principal floor. Toilet. Parking and access to rear of house

🏪 🍽 (60 plus additional 50 by arrangement) Awarded 3 stars by 'Taste of Scotland'.

📷 **F** **P** **E**

➡ Off M77 junctions 1 or 2, follow signs for Burrell Collection, 3m S of Glasgow's city centre. On National Cycle Routes 7 and 75. Frequent bus and rail (Pollokshaws West station 200 metres from Country Park entrance) from Glasgow city centre; tel (0870) 6082608. Shuttle bus from Country Park entrance to Pollok House and Burrell Collection

Pollok Country Park
🐕 Dogs on leads

🪑 👶 🚶 **R**

POLLOK HOUSE

Pollok Country Park, 2060 Pollokshaws Road, Glasgow G43 1AT.
Tel (0141) 616 6410; fax (0141) 616 6521;
email pollokhouse@nts.org.uk

Visit Pollok House and capture the flavour of one of Scotland's grandest Edwardian country houses. It is the ancestral home of the Maxwells of Pollok, who have lived on this site for 700 years. The present house, which replaced three earlier structures, was begun in 1747. It was extended from 1890 by Sir John Stirling Maxwell Bt, KT, a founder member of The National Trust for Scotland.

The house contains much original furniture as well as some of the finest Spanish paintings in Britain. A rare survival is the magnificent suite of servants' quarters, which shows the scale of country house life around 1900. These contain the popular Edwardian Kitchen Restaurant, renowned for its lunch menu and home baking, and the shop in the Housekeeper's Room. At weekends, visitors can see a reconstruction of the way the house might have been run at the turn of the last century.

Pollok House, set amid formal and walled gardens, is at the heart of Pollok Country Park, with the Burrell Collection nearby – a wonderful combination for a day out.

Sir John Stirling Maxwell placed the 458-ha (1,150-a) estate under the protection of the first Conservation Agreement of the Trust, of which he was a founder member. The house, together with its internationally famed collections, was gifted to the City of Glasgow in 1966 by Mrs Anne Maxwell Macdonald. The Trust was invited to manage the house in partnership with Glasgow City Council from 1 May 1998; the Gardens, Country Park and The Burrell Collection continue to be managed and maintained by the City Council: tel (0141) 287 2550.

OPEN	House, shop and restaurant, all year, daily 10-5. (closed 25/26 Dec and 1/2 Jan)	Gardens, Country Park and Burrell Collection all year, daily.

Entrance Hall

<Pollok House

<The Tenement House

Weaver's Cottage

20TH ANNIVERSARY EVENTS

THE TENEMENT HOUSE

145 Buccleuch Street, Garnethill, Glasgow G3 6QN.
Tel (0141) 333 0183; email tenementhouse@nts.org.uk

Glasgow, more than any Scottish city, is associated with tenements. This first-floor flat is a typical late Victorian example, consisting of four rooms and retaining most of its original features such as its bed recesses, kitchen range, coal bunker and bathroom. The furniture, furnishings and personal possessions of Miss Agnes Toward, who lived here for over fifty years, present a fascinating picture of domestic life at the beginning of the 20th century.

Special events in 2003 to celebrate 20 years of opening under Trust ownership.

The Trust restored the first-floor flat after purchasing it in 1982 from the actress Anna Davidson, who had carefully preserved its antique atmosphere after discovering it and buying it seven years earlier. Two flats on the ground floor provide reception, interpretive and educational facilities.

OPEN	I Mar to 31 Oct, daily 1-5; weekday morning visits available for pre-booked educational and other groups.

WEAVER'S COTTAGE

The Cross, Kilbarchan, Renfrewshire, PA10 2JG. Tel (01505) 705588.

This typical handloom weaver's cottage, built in 1723, houses the last of the 800 looms working in this village in the 1830s, now in use again to weave traditional fabrics. Visitors, especially children, are welcome to try the old skills of weaving, pirn winding and spinning. Upstairs, locally woven shawls cover the box beds, and 19th-century domestic items present an appealing display. Plants and herbs used to make natural dyes are a feature of the attractive cottage garden. DVD presentation on the village's links with the production of Paisley shawls.

Given in 1954 by the family of Miss Christie, the last handloom weaver in the house.

OPEN	I Apr to 30 Sep; morning visits available for pre-booked groups.

A Band D: see back flap

L Guidebook in French, German and Italian (co-financed by the European Regional Development Fund). Explanatory text in French and German

Access difficult

Braille guidebook, audio tour

P On-street parking at meters nearby, and within walking distance of city centre

→ 3rd left off Rose St or Cambridge St, NW of Sauchiehall St pedestrian shopping area (routes avoiding steep hills). 1m from National Cycle Routes 7 and 75. Cowcaddens Underground station and Charing Cross rail station ½m

A Band D: see back flap

L Explanatory text in French, German, Italian, Japanese, Spanish

Access difficult

Braille information sheet

Subtitled video

E

→ M8 junction 28A, A737, follow signs for Kilbarchan. 12m SW of Glasgow. 1m from National Cycle Routes 7 and 75. Bus: frequent service from Paisley, Glasgow and from Johnstone rail station (2m) passes door; tel (0870) 6082608

visit www.nts.org.uk

ARGYLL, BUTE & LOCH LOMOND

∧ *Crarae Garden*

In this exceptionally beautiful corner of western Scotland, the renowned tourist highlights are rapidly succeeded by tranquil less-frequented landscapes. Ben Lomond is the most visible landmark in the new Loch Lomond and the Trossachs National Park, the first to be established in Scotland.

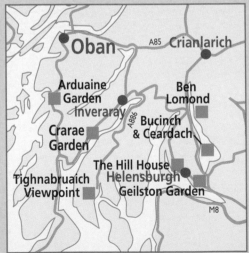

Oban
A85 Crianlarich
Arduaine Garden
Ben Lomond
Inveraray
A886
Bucinch & Ceardach
Crarae Garden
The Hill House
Helensburgh
Tighnabruaich Viewpoint
Geilston Garden
M8

For more information contact
The National Trust for Scotland
WEST REGION
Greenbank House
Flenders Road, Clarkston
Glasgow G76 8RB
Tel (0141) 616 2266

visit www.nts.org.uk

Arduaine Garden

Ben Lomond

ARDUAINE GARDEN

Arduaine, Oban, Argyll PA34 4XQ. Tel/fax (01852) 200366.

A green oasis of tranquillity nestling on the west coast, Arduaine will surprise and delight the visitor every day of the year. This 8-ha (20-a) garden on the Sound of Jura lies on the south slope of a promontory between Loch Melfort and Asknish Bay and benefits from the warming effect of the North Atlantic Drift or Gulf Stream. The spectacular rhododendrons bring enthusiasts from far and wide, and azaleas, magnolias and many other shrubs fill the garden with scent and colour. Blue Tibetan poppies, giant Himalayan lilies and Chatham Island forget-me-nots are just part of a perennial collection flowering well on into autumn. From the tall trees of the woodland garden to the water lilies in the ponds, Arduaine takes the visitor on a horticultural journey across the temperate world. Reception Centre.

James Arthur Campbell began planting in 1898, influenced by Osgood MacKenzie, creator of Inverewe, Essex nurserymen Edmund and Harry Wright bought Arduaine in 1971, and after 21 years' restoration and development gave the garden to the Trust in 1992.

OPEN	All year, daily, 9.30-sunset.	Reception Centre, 1 Apr to 30 Sep, daily 9.30-4.30

BEN LOMOND

**Ardess Lodge, Rowardennan, by Drymen, G63 0AR.
Tel (01360) 870224; email benlomond@nts.org.uk**

Rising from the east shore of Loch Lomond to a height of 974 m (3,193 ft), the Ben offers exhilarating walking and spectacular views in the heart of the Loch Lomond & the Trossachs National Park. The property, comprising 2,173 ha (5,369 a), also includes the summits of Ptarmigan, 731m (2,397 ft), Sròn Aonaich, 577 m (1,892 ft), and Beinn Uird, 596 m (1,954 ft). An extensive repair programme has brought under control what was a major path erosion scar, and walkers can help by keeping to the surfaced path. Reductions in sheep numbers, and fenced enclosures on the lower slopes, are allowing the regeneration of woodland and upland heath habitats. Ranger Centre at Ardess. New information centre/toilet facility at Rowardennan car park, run and staffed by the Loch Lomond & the Trossachs National Park, Scotland's first National Park, as of July 2002.

The property, along with adjacent Forestry Commission land, was designated the Ben Lomond National Memorial Park in December 1995, to be held in perpetuity as a tribute to those who gave their lives in the service of their country, and is to be managed primarily with conservation principles in mind. It was formally opened by the Rt Hon Donald Dewar, then Secretary of State for Scotland, on 11 November 1997. The property was purchased in 1984. The Countryside Ranger Centre at Ardess Lodge was created in 1997.

OPEN	All year, daily.

A Band D: see back flap

L Brief information sheet in French, German

& Most of garden. Wheelchair available. Toilet. Accessible path from car park (with assistance)

Y Meals and refreshments at Loch Melfort Hotel adjacent to Trust car park; tel (01852) 200233

P E

→ A816, 20m S of Oban and 18m N of Lochgilphead. Bus: infrequent service passes garden entrance; tel West Coast Motors, (01586) 552319

& Toilets and parking at Rowardennan car park. Car access to Ranger Centre on request. Some of Centre accessible

↟ Sheep-farming area, so keep dogs under control at all times

R P

→ B837, at Rowardennan, 11 miles beyond Drymen off A811. Near National Cycle Route 7. Bus: Glasgow-Drymen-Balmaha then 7m walk/cycle to Rowardennan; tel (0870) 6082608

Key to Symbols
Please refer to the inside back flap of this guide for the key to symbols and price band information. Open out for easy reference.

Bucinch & Ceardach

Crarae Garden>

Enquiries to Ben Lomond
ranger/naturalist;
tel (01360) 870224.

BUCINCH & CEARDACH
Loch Lomond.

These two small uninhabited islands, between Luss and Balmaha, were
presented by Col Charles L Spencer of Warmanbie, Dumfries, in 1943.

OPEN	All year, daily.

A Band D: see back flap

♿ Limited and in lower garden
only. Visitor Centre, shop,
refreshments accessible.
Toilet. Parking within 10
metres of Visitor Centre

🛍 ☕ **P** ⚘

→ A83, 10m S of Inveraray.
Bus: infrequent services from
Inveraray and Lochgilphead
pass garden entrance;
tel West Coast Motors,
(01586) 552319

CRARAE GARDEN   NEW
Crarae, Inveraray, Argyll PA32 8YA.
Tel/fax (Visitor Centre) (01546) 886614; or (01852) 200366

The main garden at Crarae is unique, with a strong 'sense of place'. Set
on a hillside down which tumbles the Crarae Burn, the scene is
reminiscent of a Himalayan gorge. The surrounding tree and shrub
collections are rich and diverse, planted for artistic and naturalistic effect.
The garden contains one of the best collections of the genus
Rhododendron in Scotland, unusually rich in cultivars, as well as part of the
National Collection of *Nothofagus* and particularly good representations
of *Acer*, *Eucalyptus*, *Eucryphia* and *Sorbus*. The autumn colours of the
leaves and berries are a perfect balance to the earlier blooming
rhododendrons and azaleas.

Extending to around 25 hectares, the garden was traditionally accessed
by a network of paths that criss-crossed the burn via a series of
footbridges. The Trust intends to reinstate these routes as part of a
phased programme of repairs to allow visitors full access once again.

*Lady Grace Campbell, aunt of the Himalayan plant-hunter Reginald Farrer, began the development of Crarae
Garden from woodland in 1912, on land owned by the Campbell family since 1825. Her son Sir George inherited
the estate in 1925 and lived there until 1967, greatly extending the plant collection. His son, Sir Ilay Campbell,
carried on this work, then generously gave the garden to the Crarae Garden Charitable Trust in 1978. The garden
was forced to close in 2001 following financial difficulties, but after a successful £1.5m fundraising appeal to save it
for the nation, The National Trust for Scotland was delighted to accept ownership of the garden in April 2002.*

OPEN	Garden, all year, daily 9.30-sunset. Visitor Centre, 1 Apr to 30 Sep, daily 10-5.

For public transport
information
**Tel Traveline Scotland
(0870) 6082608**

visit www.nts.org.uk

Geilston Garden>

GEILSTON GARDEN

Cardross, Dumbarton, G82 5HD.
Tel (01389) 849187; fax (01389) 849189.

This delightful garden, laid out over 200 years ago, has many interesting features. The house (not open to the public) is thought to date from the late 17th century. The garden retains a sense of private space into which the visitor is invited. The walled garden is laid out with shrub borders, lawns and a herbaceous border that provides summer colour on a grand scale. Fruit, vegetables and cut flowers are grown in the kitchen garden and the Geilston Burn winds its way through enchanting woodland walks.

Bequeathed to the Trust by Miss E C Hendry in 1989 with a generous endowment.

OPEN	1 Apr to 31 Oct, daily 9.30-5. House not open.

A Band E: see back flap

& Access throughout, except to part of walled garden and steep or uneven paths in glen and woodland. Toilet

→ On A814 at west end of Cardross, 18m NW of Glasgow. 3m from National Cycle Route 7.
Bus: hourly service Helensburgh-Dumbarton passes entrance to drive; or ½-hourly train service to Cardross station (1m): tel (0870) 6082608

Crarae Garden

Key to Symbols
Please refer to the inside back flap of this guide for the key to symbols and price band information. Open out for easy reference.

The Hill House>

THE HILL HOUSE
Upper Colquhoun Street, Helensburgh G84 9AJ.
Tel (01436) 673900; fax (01436) 674685.

The finest of Charles Rennie Mackintosh's domestic creations, The Hill House sits high above the Clyde, commanding fine views over the river estuary. Walter Blackie, director of the well-known Glasgow publishers, commissioned not only the house and garden but much of the furniture and all the interior fittings and decorative schemes. Mackintosh's wife, Margaret MacDonald, contributed fabric designs and a unique gesso overmantel. The overall effect is daring, but restrained in its elegance: the result, timeless rooms, as modern today as they must have been in 1904 when the Blackie family moved in. An information room interprets the special relationship between architect and patron and provides a historical context for *Inspirations*, a dazzling exhibition in the upper east wing and the gardens. It brings together exceptional pieces of domestic design by great living designers, all of whom, in some way, pay homage to Mackintosh's elegance and invention. Inspiring comparisons may be drawn between the work of Mackintosh, now recognised as one of the geniuses of the early 20th century, and pieces that themselves have become 21st-century icons.

The gardens have been restored to their former glory, and reflect features common to Mackintosh's architectural designs. They also contain a kinetic sculpture given to the house by the artist George Rickey.

The Hill House came into the care of the Trust in June 1982 when it accepted the offer of the building from The Hill House Trustees with the approval of the Royal Incorporation of Architects in Scotland.

OPEN	1 Apr to 31 Oct, daily 1.30-5.30. Groups should pre-book.	Weekday morning visits available for pre-booked groups.

TIGHNABRUAICH VIEWPOINT
Argyll & Bute.

The indicators, attributed to the Trust and the Scottish Civic Trust, were erected by a Trust supporter in memory of two brothers, who gave generously of their time to the work of the Trust.

OPEN	All year, daily.

The National Trust for Scotland

CENTRAL SCOTLAND

The setting for some of Scotland's finest landscapes and most turbulent history, of which perhaps the most significant monument is the battle site of Bannockburn, vividly interpreted at the Trust's Heritage Centre.

Bannockburn

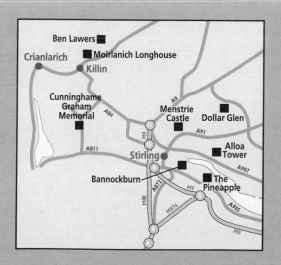

Ben Lawers
Crianlarich
Moirlanich Longhouse
Killin
Cunninghame Graham Memorial
A84
Menstrie Castle
A9
Dollar Glen
A91
A811
M9
Stirling
Alloa Tower
A907
Bannockburn
A872
The Pineapple
M9
M80
M876
A905
M9

For more information contact
The National Trust for Scotland
WEST REGION
Greenbank House
Flenders Road, Clarkston
Glasgow G76 8RB
Tel (0141) 616 2266

visit www.nts.org.uk

Alloa Tower>

A Band D: see back flap (25% discount to Clackmannanshire residents)

Toilet. Ground floor only. Slides of portraits in Tower on ground floor. Parking at door by arrangement

Audio tour

F P E ⚬

Off A907, in Alloa, close to town centre. 1m from National Cycle Route 76. Bus: stops in town centre, then short walk; tel Mackie's Coaches, (01259) 216180.

Key to Symbols
Please refer to the inside back flap of this guide for the key to symbols and price band information. Open out for easy reference.

ALLOA TOWER
Alloa Park, Alloa, Clackmannanshire, FK10 1PP.
Tel (01259) 211701; fax (01259) 218744.

Alloa Tower, the largest surviving keep in Scotland, dates from the 14th century. It was home to successive generations of the Earls of Mar, who played host to and were guardians of many Scots monarchs. Here, so legend has it, Mary, Queen of Scots was reconciled with Darnley and shortly thereafter granted the 5th Lord Erskine the much-coveted earldom in 1565. One tradition holds that Mary's infant son, later James VI and I, died shortly after his birth and was replaced by the baby son of the Earl of Mar.

The Tower has seen six major alterations, the most dramatic being the sweeping Italianate staircase and dome added in the early 1700s by the 6th Earl of Mar. But it still retains original medieval features such as the dungeon, first-floor well and magnificent oak roof timbers. Fully restored and furnished to a high standard, the Tower contains a unique collection of family portraits and silver on loan from the present Earl of Mar and Kellie.

In 1988, the 13th Earl of Mar and Kellie and Clackmannan District Council formed the Alloa Tower Building Preservation Trust, which has carried out an eight-year restoration programme that recently received a Civic Trust award. Alloa Tower is now being managed by the NTS in partnership with Clackmannanshire Council, and is in the process of being transferred to the NTS by the current trustees. The Tower was officially opened by Her Majesty the Queen in July 1997 to mark its 500th anniversary.

OPEN	1 Apr to 31 Oct, daily 1-5. Weekday morning visits available for pre-booked groups.

Ben Lawers

<Bannockburn>

BANNOCKBURN

Glasgow Road, Stirling FK7 0LJ.
Tel (01786) 812664; fax (01786) 810892.

The Bannockburn Heritage Centre is situated at one of the most important historic sites in Scotland. On the battlefield nearby, in June 1314, King Robert the Bruce routed the forces of King Edward II to win freedom for the Scots from English domination. Near the Centre is the famous Borestone site which by tradition was Bruce's command post before the battle; it is marked by an impressive equestrian statue of Bruce by Pilkington Jackson. The Centre contains an exhibition on the period of the battle, and an audio-visual presentation.

In 1930, to prevent use of the ground for building, a committee under the 10th Earl of Elgin and Kincardine, head of the Bruce family, raised funds to purchase 23 ha (57 a) of the Borestone area. This was subsequently presented to the Trust which in 1960 purchased further land, facilitating access from M80 and M9 via A872.

OPEN	Site, all year, daily.	Heritage Centre, shop and café, 1 Feb to 31 Mar and 1 Nov to 24 Dec, daily 10.30-4; 1 Apr to 31 Oct, daily 10-5.30 (last audio-visual show half-an-hour before closing).

A Band D: see back flap (includes audio tour)

L Guidebook in French and German; A/V in French and German for groups

Site, Heritage Centre and audio-visual presentation. Toilet. Wheelchair available. Parking at Centre

Braille guidebook

Induction loop for the hard-of-hearing in A/V theatre

(60)

F P Band H

→ Off M80/M9 at Junction 9, on A872 2m S of Stirling. Bus: from Stirling bus station. Guide Friday Heritage Tour bus, Apr-Sep

BEN LAWERS NATIONAL NATURE RESERVE

Scotland's National Nature Reserves

NTS Office, Lynedoch, Main Street, Killin FK21 8UW.
Tel (01567) 820397 (Information Centre) or
tel/fax (01567) 820988 (office) (Mon-Fri 9-3).

The central Highlands' highest mountain, Ben Lawers is 1,214 m (3,984 ft), with views from the Atlantic to the North Sea. In the Trust's care are 3,374 ha (8,339 a) of the southern slopes of the Lawers range and 1,348 ha (3,331 a) of the Tarmachan range, noted for a rich variety of mountain plants and including Meall nan Tarmachan (1,044 m, 3,425 ft). Birds include raven, ring-ouzel, red grouse, ptarmigan, dipper and curlew. Nature trail and other areas fenced to exclude sheep and deer to allow the restoration of trees, shrubs and herbaceous plants; projects include pioneering work to restore treeline woodland habitats. Audio-visual programmes with special version for children.

Bought in 1950 by the Trust's Mountainous Country Fund formed by Percy Unna. The Tarmachan range was bought in 1996. The Mountain Visitor Centre was opened in 1972. In 1975 the area was declared a National Nature Reserve. It is now managed with financial support from Scottish Natural Heritage.

OPEN	Site, all year, daily.	Information Centre and shop, 1 Apr to 30 Sep, daily 10-5 (may close for half-an-hour between 1 and 2.)

A Band G: see back flap

Information Centre and shop Toilet

Dogs not allowed in Information Centre, and on hill must be kept on lead at all times

R

P Mountain Band H: see back flap. Information Centre free in public car parks nearby

E

→ Information Centre and shop, Lynedoch, Main Street, Killin. Mountain car park off A827, 6m NE of Killin, N of Loch Tay. Near National Cycle Route 7

Dollar Glen

Menstrie Castle

Cunninghame Graham Memorial

→ Off A81, in Gartmore,
2½m SW of Aberfoyle.
On National Cycle Route 7

CUNNINGHAME GRAHAM MEMORIAL
Gartmore, Stirling.

Cairn to the memory of R B Cunninghame Graham of Ardoch,
distinguished Scottish author, politician and traveller; erected in 1937, one
year after his death, at Castlehill, Dumbarton. Moved to Gartmore in 1981.

OPEN	All year, daily.

Enquiries to
West Regional Office;
tel (0141) 616 2266.

🐕 Dogs must be kept strictly
under control for safety
reasons and on leads
during lambing season
in spring and summer

🚶 📖

→ Off A91, in Dollar. Bus:
regular service from Stirling;
tel (01324) 613777

DOLLAR GLEN
Dollar, Clackmannanshire.

This wooded glen provides spectacular walks to Castle Campbell
(see page 84). 22 ha (54 a). During or after rain the paths can be
dangerous; great care is advised. Dollar Glen was designated as a
Site of Special Scientific Interest in 1989 on account of its range of
diverse habitats and important geological features.

Glen and castle given by the late Mr J E Kerr, CBE, of Harviestoun in 1950.

OPEN	All year, daily.

Enquiries to
Alloa Tower, Alloa Park, Alloa,
Clackmannanshire FK10 1PP;
tel (01259) 211701.

🅰 Free

→ Off A91, in Menstrie,
5m NE of Stirling

MENSTRIE CASTLE
Castle Street, Menstrie, Clackmannanshire.

The castle is not Trust property but the Trust, in co-operation with the
then Clackmannanshire County Council, played a large part in saving it
from demolition. It was the birthplace of Sir William Alexander, James VI's
Lieutenant for the Plantation of Nova Scotia, and an exhibition in the
Nova Scotia Commemoration Room tells the story of this ill-fated scheme.

OPEN	Easter Sunday and 1 May to 30 Sep, Wed and Sun 2-5.

Dollar Glen

Moirlanich Longhouse

The Pineapple

MOIRLANICH LONGHOUSE
Near Killin, Stirling.

An outstanding example of a traditional cruck frame cottage and byre, dating from the mid-19th century. The building has been little altered and retains many of its original features, such as the 'hingin' lum' and box beds. Moirlanich was home to at least three generations of the Robertson family: the last member left in 1968. The cottage is furnished according to archaeological evidence. A small adjacent building displays a rare collection of working and 'Sunday best' clothes found n the Longhouse, and an exhibition interprets the history and restoration of the building.

Purchased in 1997, following a generous donation in memory of Sheriff Prain, from his family.

OPEN	Easter Sunday and 1 May to 30 Sep, Wed and Sun 2-5.

THE PINEAPPLE
N of Airth, Falkirk. Tel (01324) 831137.

A bizarre structure in the shape of a pineapple, 14 m (45 ft) high, built in 1761 as a garden retreat. The policies, now an oasis for wildlife, including bats and the great crested newt, include a car park, pond and woodland. An orchard of crab-apple trees has been planted in the walled garden. The Trust maintains the gardens and policies; the building is leased to the Landmark Trust.

Given with 6.5 ha (16 a) of gardens and policies by the Countess of Perth in 1974. Acceptance made possible by the co-operation of the Landmark Trust, which has leased and restored the building and walls, creating a holiday home. Enquiries for short lets to: Landmark Trust, Shottesbrooke, Maidenhead, Berks. Tel (01628) 825925.

OPEN	Grounds, all year, daily 9.30-sunset

Staffed by volunteers from Killin Heritage Society. Enquiries to NTS Office, Lynedoch, Main Street, Killin, FK21 8UW; tel/fax (01567) 820988 (Mon-Fri 9-3).

A Band F: see back flap

&. Reception building, but not Longhouse. Toilet

P Limited car parking: access unsuitable for coaches

→ On Glen Lochay Road, off A827, 1m NW of Killin. 1m from National Cycle Route 7

✳

→ 7m E of Stirling, off A905, then off B9124. 1m W of Airth

Key to Symbols
Please refer to the inside back flap of this guide for the key to symbols and price band information. Open out for easy reference.

visit www.nts.org.uk

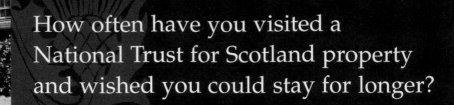

How often have you visited a National Trust for Scotland property and wished you could stay for longer?

Well, you can! The Trust has fifty holiday properties across Scotland, ranging from cottages on Highland country estates to remote crofts on the Isle of Skye, from wings of castles and a shooting lodge in the Cairngorms to apartments in Edinburgh's historic city centre.

All accommodation is maintained to a high standard and we are winning many 'Green' Tourism Business Scheme awards, which places an onus on the Trust to run the accommodation in an environmentally sensitive way. Whether your interest lies in hillwalking, sailing, visiting historic houses, castles and distilleries, 'doing' the Edinburgh Festival or enjoying a romantic break in a secluded Gothic lodge, the Trust has something for everyone. Many properties are furnished with fine antiques and, where possible, we have kept open log fires. Selected properties are fully equipped with cots, toddler gates and full child safety equipment.

The properties sleep between two and thirty people, and are available for short breaks as well as full weeks. A number of them are open all year: if you would like to book a Christmas or New Year break, get in touch well before the festive season, since this is a very popular time.

For keen walkers and lovers of the great outdoors, Base Camps are available in remoter areas such as Torridon and Canna and, as the name suggests, are situated near spectacular walking country. They provide comfortable facilities to give you the best start to that energetic day on the hills. Our Base Camps sleep between ten and twenty.

Call us on (0131) 243 9331, or email holidays@nts.org.uk We'll be delighted to send you a copy of our brochure, and we accept bookings for 2004 as well as 2003!

The National Trust for Scotland

PERTHSHIRE

Magnificent gateway to the Highlands, this region's wooded gorges and tumbling rivers are at their most spectacular in autumn. At Killiecrankie, rich in wildlife and site of the first battle between the government and the Jacobites, costumed guides bring the story to life.

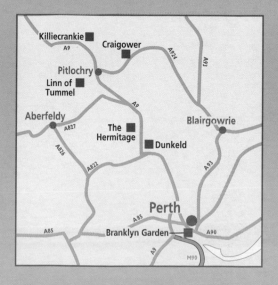

Killiecrankie

**For more information contact
The National Trust for Scotland
NORTH-EAST REGION**
The Stables
Castle Fraser, Sauchen
Inverurie AB51 7LD
Tel (01330) 833225

visit www.nts.org.uk

Branklyn Garden>

A Band C: see back flap

♿ About ⅓ of garden. Toilets. Wheelchair available. Parking at entrance, by arrangement with shop staff

🛍 ✻ 📷📖

P Car park 400 metres downhill from entrance

➡ A85, Dundee Road, north of Perth over Queen's Bridge. From north via A90, ½mile from junction with A85. Bus: Stagecoach (No 16) Perth-Dundee service, stops 200 metres from garden; tel (01738) 629339. Rail: Perth station 25 mins' walk; tel (08457) 484950

Senior ranger/naturalist: Ben Notley

🚶 R ❄

➡ Off A924 at Moulin, 1½m N of Pitlochry. 1m from National Cycle Route 7

BRANKLYN GARDEN

116 Dundee Road, Perth PH2 7BB. Tel (01738) 625535.

This attractive little garden, a haven of peace within walking distance of Perth, was once described as 'the finest two acres of private garden in the country'. It contains an outstanding collection of plants, particularly rhododendrons, alpines, herbaceous and peat-garden plants, which attracts gardeners and botanists from all over the world. One of the most breathtaking of the unusual plants here is the vivid blue *Meconopsis* (Himalayan poppy).

It was bequeathed to the Trust in 1967 by John T Renton, CBE who, with his wife, began the garden planting in 1922, on the site of a former orchard.

OPEN	1 to 30 Apr and 1 Jul to 30 Sep, Fri-Tue 10-5; 1 May to 30 Jun, daily 10-5.

CRAIGOWER

Near Pitlochry, Perth & Kinross. Tel (01350) 728641 (Ranger Office) or tel/fax (01796) 473233 (Killiecrankie Visitor Centre).

A 4.5-ha (11-a) beacon hill with splendid views. The path from the small car park to the summit has been extended to form the Dunmore Trail in memory of John, Earl of Dunmore (1939-80), member of NTS Council and Executive Committee, and of his father, the Viscount Fincastle, who was killed in action in 1940.

Given in 1947 by Mrs M D Fergusson of Baledmund in memory of her father, Capt G A K Wisely.

OPEN	All year, daily.

<Craigower

Dunkeld

The Hermitage

DUNKELD

Ell Shop, The Cross, Dunkeld, Perth & Kinross, PH8 0AN.
Tel (01350) 727460; email dunkeld@nts.org.uk

The Trust owns 20 houses in The Cross and Cathedral Street; most date from the rebuilding of the town after the Battle of Dunkeld in 1689. Restored by the Trust, the houses provide homes of modern standards while retaining the charm of their period exteriors. Although these private homes are not open to the public, visitors are welcome at the Trust's Ell Shop, which takes its name from the ell or weaver's measure fixed to the wall outside. The Atholl Memorial Fountain at the centre of the Cross was restored to working order in 1993.

Stanley Hill, a fragment of the designed landscape for Dunkeld House, laid out in 1730 by the Duke of Atholl. The mound itself has an ice-house, reached by steps. 2.4 ha (6 a). Maintained by Perth and Kinross Council.

Banks of Tay and Braan. The south banks of the River Tay and the River Braan, from the Inver Road to the Inchewen Burn, form part of the Birnam Circular Walk.

The original group of houses was presented by Atholl Estates in 1954; Stanley Hill by Messrs J Jones (Larbert) Ltd in 1958. River banks presented by the Duke of Atholl in 1985. The Atholl Memorial Fountain was given to the Trust in 1989.

OPEN	Ell Shop, 22 Mar to 30 Sep, Mon-Sat 10-5.30, Sun 12.30-5.30; 1 Oct to 24 Dec, Mon-Sat 10-4.30, Sun 12.30-4.30.

♿ Ell Shop. Ground floor of Tourist Information Centre. Toilets 25 yards

Subtitled video in Tourist Information Centre

→ Off A9, 15m N of Perth. On National Cycle Route 77. Bus: Stagecoach; tel (01738) 629339. Rail: Dunkeld & Birnam station 1m; tel (08457) 484950

THE HERMITAGE

Perth & Kinross. Tel (01350) 728641 (Ranger Office)
or tel/fax (01796) 473233 (Killiecrankie Visitor Centre);
email hermitage@nts.org.uk

Ideal for walks, these 13 ha (33 a) of interesting mixed conifer and deciduous woodlands contain one of Britain's tallest Douglas fir trees, and are especially spectacular in autumn. Above the wooded gorge of the River Braan is a picturesque folly – 'Ossian's Hall' – built in 1758 and restored in 1952.

By the wish of the 8th Duke of Atholl, first president of the Trust, presented by his widow, Katharine, Duchess of Atholl, in 1944.

OPEN	All year, daily.

♿ Car park at Ossian's Hall for disabled badge holders

P Band H: see back flap

R Details from Dunkeld shop or Killiecrankie Visitor Centre

E

→ Off A9, 2m W of Dunkeld. 1m from National Cycle Route 77. Bus: request stop at Inver; tel Stagecoach, (01738) 629339

<Killiecrankie   Linn of Tummel

L Guidebook in French and German. Explanatory text in Danish, French, Gaelic, German, Italian, Japanese, Swedish

& Visitor Centre, with viewing balcony, shop. Carry-out refreshments only, so assistance necessary. Toilet. Parking at Centre. Wheelchair available.

Braille guidebook

P Band H: see back flap

➡ B8079, 3m N of Pitlochry. On National Cycle Route 7. Bus: Elizabeth Yule local service from Pitlochry; tel (01796) 472290

KILLIECRANKIE

Pitlochry, Perth & Kinross, PH16 5LG.
Tel/fax (01796) 473233 (Visitor Centre)
or (01350) 728641 (Ranger Office); email killiecrankie@nts.org.uk

On 27 July 1689, the Pass of Killiecrankie echoed with the sound of battle cries and gunfire when, nearby, a Jacobite army led by 'Bonnie Dundee' defeated the government forces. One soldier evaded capture by making a spectacular jump across the River Garry at Soldier's Leap. The magnificent wooded gorge, much admired by Queen Victoria in 1844, is tranquil now, and is designated a Site of Special Scientific Interest because it is a fine example of an oak and mixed deciduous woodland.

The Visitor Centre exhibition features the battle, natural history and ranger services. In the Centre, visitors can now watch birds nesting, via a remote camera in the woodlands.

The 16 ha (40 a) of the Pass of Killiecrankie, formerly part of the estate of Faskally, came to the Trust in 1947 by a gift from Edith Foster.

OPEN	Site, all year, daily.	Visitor Centre, shop and snack-bar, 1 Apr to 30 Jun and 1 Sep to 31 Oct, daily 10-5.30; 1 Jul to 31 Aug, daily 9.30-6.

P At Garry Bridge

➡ B8019, 2½m NW of Pitlochry. 1m from National Cycle Route 7. Bus: Elizabeth Yule local service from Pitlochry to Garry Bridge; tel (01796) 472290

LINN OF TUMMEL

Perth & Kinross. Tel/fax (01796) 473233 (Killiecrankie Visitor Centre)
or (01350) 728641 (Ranger Office).

Characteristic of the beauty of the Perthshire Highlands, the Linn of Tummel comprises 16 ha (40 a) by the banks of the Rivers Tummel and Garry and is adjacent to the Trust's Killiecrankie property. A path through mixed woodland leads to the Linn of Tummel. An obelisk commemorates a visit by Queen Victoria in 1844. At that time the Tummel made a plunging fall to join the Garry. The fall became the Linn (Gaelic – linne, a pool) when the level of both rivers was raised in 1950 by the creation of Loch Faskally in a hydro-electric scheme. Beside the Linn is a very early example of a fish-pass which previously had enabled salmon to bypass the falls.

Given by Dr G F Barbour of Bonskeid in 1944.

For public transport information
Tel Traveline Scotland (0870) 6082608

OPEN	All year, daily.

The National Trust for Scotland

ANGUS

Successive invasions over the centuries have given this area a rich heritage, with important historic sites. The exquisite House of Dun, designed by William Adam, and perched on the rim of the Montrose Basin, is perhaps the most impressively sited of the noble houses of Angus.

In 2004, join the centenary celebrations of the publication of *Peter Pan* at the birthplace of his creator, J M Barrie.

House of Dun

**For more information contact
The National Trust for Scotland
NORTH-EAST REGION**
The Stables
Castle Fraser, Sauchen
Inverurie AB51 7LD
Tel (01330) 833225

visit www.nts.org.uk

Angus Folk Museum>

ANGUS FOLK MUSEUM
Kirkwynd, Glamis, Forfar, Angus DD8 1RT. Tel (01307) 840288.

Housing one of Scotland's finest folk collections, this museum presents a vivid insight into how the rural workforce used to live. Six charming 18th-century cottages contain the domestic section, and the agricultural collection is in the farm steading opposite, illustrating changes in the Angus countryside over the last 200 years. One of the most dramatic artifacts is the restored 19th-century black horse-drawn 'Glenisla' hearse.

This collection was brought together by Jean, Lady Maitland, and was previously the responsibility of local trustees. The steading building was donated by the Earl of Strathmore and Kinghorne.

| OPEN | 1 Apr to 30 Jun and 1 to 30 Sep, Fri-Tue 12-5; 1 Jul to 31 Aug, daily 12-5. |

J M BARRIE'S BIRTHPLACE
9 Brechin Road, Kirriemuir, Angus DD8 4BX. Tel (01575) 572646.

In this two-storeyed house J M Barrie (1860-1937), the creator of *Peter Pan*, was born. The upper floors are furnished as they may have been when Barrie lived there. The adjacent house, No 11, contains an exhibition – *The Genius of J M Barrie* – about Barrie's literary and theatrical works. The outside wash-house is said to have been his first theatre. Audio programme. The garden has been redeveloped to include a living-willow crocodile, Peter Pan statue and a 'Pirates' Workshop' for schools events. In 2004, join in the centenary celebrations of the publication of *Peter Pan*.

At Barrie's death there was a proposal to remove the birthplace to the USA, but in 1937 Mr D Alves bought it and gave it to the Trust with funds for restoration.

| OPEN | 1 Apr to 30 Jun and 1 to 30 Sep, Fri-Tue 12-5; 1 Jul to 31 Aug, daily 12-5. |

J M Barrie's Birthplace>

<Barry Water Mill

Camera Obscura

BARRY WATER MILL

Barry, Carnoustie, Angus DD7 7RJ. Tel (01241) 856761.

The original machinery in this 19th-century meal mill, rebuilt in 1814 after a fire, has been fully restored and visitors can see it turning once more. Barry Mill was the last working water-powered meal mill in Angus, producing oatmeal until the late 1970s and animal feed until 1982. Records show that a mill has occupied this site since at least 1539. Milling demonstrations normally take place on Sunday afternoons and for pre booked parties. Displays highlight the important place the mill held in the community.

In 1988, the Trust bought the deteriorating buildings to prevent further decay and to conserve them for the nation.

OPEN	1 Apr to 30 Sep, Fri-Tue 12-5.

CAMERA OBSCURA

Kirrie Hill, Kirriemuir.

In 1930, J M Barrie was given the freedom of Kirriemuir. He subsequently presented the town with the cricket pavilion on Kirrie Hill, and the Camera Obscura within it. The Camera Obscura is opened in co-operation with Angus Council. (At times, it will be unable to operate due to weather conditions, which may result in closure for the whole day.)

OPEN	1 Apr to 30 Sep, daily 12-5. Last viewing 4.40.

A Band C: see back flap

♿ Toilet. Most parts accessible. Disabled visitors may alight at mill by arrangement

🐕 Dog walk

🏛 🚶 📖 **P**

➡ N of Barry village between A92 and A930, 2m W of Carnoustie. 1m from National Cycle Route 1. Bus: Strathtay Buses from Dundee, Carnoustie and Arbroath, stop in Barry village (½m); tel (01382) 228054

For enquiries
tel (01575) 572646

A Combined ticket with J M Barrie's Birthplace, Band C; when Birthplace closed, Band D: see back flap

♿ Interpretation on ground floor, but camera inaccessible

🏛 ⛰ ❀

P Free car parking adjacent to pavilion

➡ A90/A926, in Kirriemuir, 6m NW of Forfar. Signposted from Kirriemuir High Street. Bus: Strathtay Buses (No 20) from Dundee via Forfar; tel (01382) 228054

Barry Water Mill

Finavon Doocot

House of Dun>

→ Off A90, 6 miles N of Forfar

FINAVON DOOCOT
Angus.

Largest doocot in Scotland, with 2,400 nesting boxes. Believed to have been built by the Earl of Crawford in the 16th century.

Passed into the care of the Trust by the Angus Historic Buildings Society in 1993.

OPEN	All year, daily. Keys from Finavon Hotel.

A Band B; garden and grounds only, Band G: see back flap

L Explanatory text in French and German

& East walled garden, terrace and courtyard. Basement rooms at ground level; stairlift to ground floor. Toilet. Wheelchair available. Parking in courtyard. Access to Basin but not to foreshore

👁 Braille information sheets

🔲 Subtitled video

🐕 Dog walk in woodland

🎣 Salmon fishings available on River South Esk. Season 16 Feb to 31 Oct. Full details, rod charges and booking conditions from Property Manager

🏠 ✖ (36)

 🎈 🕴 📖 **F R P**

E ☀ ✹

→ On A935, 3m W of Montrose. 3m from National Cycle Route 1.
Bus: Strathtay Buses; tel (01382) 228054

HOUSE OF DUN & MONTROSE BASIN NATURE RESERVE
Montrose, Angus, DD10 9LQ. Tel (01674) 810264; fax (01674) 810722; email houseofdun@nts.org.uk

Georgian house overlooking the Montrose Basin, designed and built by William Adam in 1730 for David Erskine, Lord Dun. Superb contemporary plasterwork by Joseph Enzer. Lady Augusta Kennedy-Erskine was the daughter of William IV and Mrs Jordan, and the house contains royal mementos of that period and many examples of Lady Augusta's woolwork and embroidery. Family collection of portraits, furniture and porcelain. Miniature theatre display and video.

Courtyard buildings include a handloom weaving workshop. The small walled garden has been largely restored to a late Victorian period and includes a range of plants typical of the 1880s. A wooded den, first planted in the 19th century, contains a plum-pudding rock garden, a selection of evergreen shrubs and woodland plants.

The Trust owns much of the western half of the Montrose Basin Local Nature Reserve, which is farmed in an environmentally sensitive manner: in 2003 a large area of wetland will be restored. It is internationally important for its wildfowl and geese, and offers interpretation, waymarked paths and observation hides. Access from the House on foot or from the Old Mill car park to the south, on Bridge of Dun road. The reserve is managed by the Scottish Wildlife Trust in association with The National Trust for Scotland and Angus Council.

The property was bequeathed to the Trust in 1980 by Mrs M A A Lovett. There is a tenanted farm, woodlands and cottages comprising 368 ha (909 a).

OPEN	House, shop and restaurant, 1 Apr to 30 Jun and 1 to 30 Sep, Fri-Tue 12-5; 1 Jul to 31 Aug, daily 12-5. Guided tours only.	Garden and grounds, all year, daily 9.30-sunset.

The National Trust for Scotland

ABERDEEN & GRAMPIAN

Pitmedden Garden

An area famous for its awesome mountains and splendidly preserved castles. Here, the Trust welcomes visitors to fine examples of Scottish Baronial architecture, most notably Crathes Castle, with its fairytale turrets and superb gardens. The *Live on the Lawn* rock concerts at Crathes are an eagerly-awaited annual highlight.

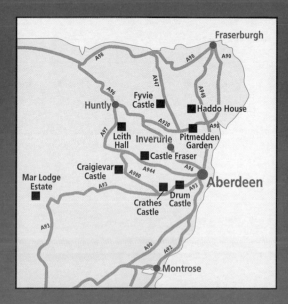

For more information contact
The National Trust for Scotland
NORTH-EAST REGION
The Stables
Castle Fraser, Sauchen
Inverurie AB51 7LD
Tel (01330) 833225

visit www.nts.org.uk

<Castle Fraser Garden & Estate>

A Castle, garden and grounds, Band B: see back flap

L Explanatory text in Dutch, French, German, Italian, Japanese, Russian, Spanish

♿ Entrance hall and tearoom only. All garden accessible. Toilet. Parking at castle

🛍

🍽 (38)

🎏 ⛩ 🛝 🧘 🌿 📖 **F**
R **P** Band H: see back flap
E ✳

➔ Off A944, 4m N of Dunecht and 16m W of Aberdeen. Bus: from Aberdeen Bus Station; tel Stagecoach Bluebird (01224) 212266

CASTLE FRASER, GARDEN & ESTATE
Sauchen, Inverurie, Aberdeenshire AB51 7LD.
Tel (01330) 833463; fax (01330) 833819;
email castlefraser@nts.org.uk. Ranger service: tel (01330) 844651.

The most elaborate Z-plan castle in Scotland, and one of the grandest Castles of Mar, Castle Fraser was built between 1575 and 1636 by the 6th laird, Michael Fraser, and was the supreme work of two great families of master masons, Bell and Leiper. The castle belongs to the same period of native architectural achievement as two neighbouring castles, Crathes and Craigievar, both owned by the Trust. One of its most evocative rooms is the strikingly simple Great Hall. The castle contains many Fraser family portraits, including one by Raeburn, and fine 18th- and 19th-century carpets, curtains and bed hangings. One of the 17th-century 'laigh biggins' now contains a shop selling exclusive gifts. The historic walled garden features shrubs, flowers, wall-trained fruit and vegetables. The estate contains a flight pond, mixed woodland and open farmland, with two waymarked walks giving magnificent views of the local hills.

The property of 10.5 ha (26 a) was given into the care of the Trust in 1976 by Major and Mrs Michael Smiley, along with an endowment. In 1993 the Trust purchased a further 127 ha (314 a) of land surrounding the castle.

OPEN	1 Apr to 30 Jun and 1 to 30 Sep, Fri-Tue 12-5.30; 1 Jul to 31 Aug, daily 11-5.30.

Castle Fraser Garden & Estate

Craigievar Castle>

CRAIGIEVAR CASTLE

Alford, Aberdeenshire, AB33 8JF. Tel (013398) 83635;
fax (013398) 83280. Ranger service: tel (01330) 844651.

This fairytale-like castle, an example of the best of Scottish Baronial
architecture, seems to have grown naturally out of the beautiful rolling
hillsides of Aberdeenshire. The Great Tower stands just as it was when
completed by Master William Forbes – 'Danzig Willie' – in 1626. The
simplicity of its lower towers contrasts perfectly with the turrets, the
cupolas and corbelling that embellish the roofline. Within its walls the
collection includes an excellent show of family portraits and 17th and
18th-century furniture. This perfect Scottish castle remains as unspoiled
as it was when lived in by the Forbes-Sempill family.

A waymarked walk leads through the policies with beautiful views of the
castle and surrounding hills.

*Craigievar Castle and some 13 ha (32 a) of ground were bought from the Forbes-Sempill family by a consortium
of benefactors and presented to the Trust in 1963. The property has since been extended by the purchase of an
additional 24 ha (60 a) of farmland providing a safeguard for its amenity.*

OPEN	1 Apr to 30 Sep, Fri-Tue 12-5.30. Guided tours only. No coaches, no groups.	Grounds, all year, daily 9.30-sunset.

A Band A: see back flap

L Explanatory text in French, German, Italian, Spanish

Access to castle very difficult. Parking at rear

P Band I: see back flap

On A980, 6m S of Alford and 26m W of Aberdeen

Key to Symbols
Please refer to the inside
back flap of this guide for
the key to symbols and price
band information. Open out
for easy reference.

Craigievar Castle

<Crathes Castle

Horsemill Restaurant;
tel (01330) 844634. Trust
shop; tel (01330) 844757.

 Castle/walled garden and
grounds only, Band B
(no family, no group rates);
combined ticket, Band A:
see back flap

L Guidebook in French and
German. Explanatory text in
Azerbaijani, Czech, Danish,
Dutch, Finnish, French,
German, Hebrew, Italian,
Japanese, Norwegian,
Polish, Portuguese, Russian,
Spanish, Swedish

♿ Ground floor of castle; garden
and grounds; viewpoint trail;
shop; exhibitions; restaurant.
Toilets. Wheelchairs available.
Parking at castle and Visitor
Centre

Audio tour of garden.
Braille guidebook

🛍

🏆 (104) 'Taste of Scotland'.

🚉 ⛰ 🧍 🌿 🐾 **F** **R**

P Band H: see back flap

E 🌿 ❄

➡ On A93, 3m E of Banchory
and 15m W of Aberdeen.
Bus: from Aberdeen Bus
Station; tel Stagecoach
Bluebird, tel (01224) 212266

To help you enjoy your
visit and for safety reasons,
admission to the castle is
by timed ticket (limited
numbers: entry may be
delayed).

CRATHES CASTLE, GARDEN & ESTATE
Banchory, Aberdeenshire AB31 5QJ.
Castle: tel (01330) 844525; fax (01330) 844797;
email crathes@nts.org.uk. Ranger service: tel (01330) 844651.

King Robert the Bruce granted the lands of Leys to the Burnett family
in 1323: the ancient Horn of Leys, which can be seen today in the
Great Hall, marks his gift. The castle, built in the second half of the
16th century, is a superb example of a tower house of the period.
Some of the rooms retain their original painted ceilings and collections
of family portraits and furniture.

A visit is enhanced by the 1.5 ha (3.75 a) of walled garden, which
incorporates herbaceous borders and many unusual plants, providing
a wonderful display at all times of the year. The great yew hedges,
fascinating examples of the art of topiary, date from as early as 1702.
Explore the estate on the seven waymarked trails (including one
suitable for wheelchairs) that lead through the mixed woodlands,
along the Coy Burn and past the millpond. In the Visitor Centre a
new exhibition, *A Walk on the Wild Side*, explores the wildlife on
the Crathes Estate.

*The property of Crathes, consisting of 215 ha (531 a) of woodland, fields and gardens, was given to the Trust in
1951 by Sir James Burnett of Leys, Bt, with an endowment.*

OPEN	Castle & Visitor Centre, 1 Apr to 30 Sep, daily 10-5.30; 1 to 31 Oct, daily 10-4.30. Restaurant and shop, 18 Jan to 31 Mar and 1 Nov to 21 Dec, Wed-Sun 10-4; 1 Apr to 30 Sep, daily 10-5.30; 1 to 31 Oct, daily 10-4.30.	Garden and grounds, all year, daily 9-sunset.

Crathes Castle Garden

<Drum Castle, Garden & Estate>

DRUM CASTLE, GARDEN & ESTATE

Drumoak, by Banchory, Aberdeenshire AB31 5EY.
Tel (01330) 811204; fax (01330) 811962; email drum@nts.org.uk
website www.drum-castle.org.uk Ranger service: tel (01330) 844651.

The keep is one of the three oldest tower houses surviving in Scotland. It was the work of Richard Cementarius, first Provost of Aberdeen and King's Master Mason, in the late 13th century. The High Hall of the tower is still in its medieval state. It is accessed by a narrow newel stair, and offers fine views from the battlements. The original house was enlarged with the creation of a very fine Jacobean mansion house in 1619 and a later addition during the reign of Queen Victoria.

William de Irwyn was given the charter of the Royal Forest of Drum by King Robert the Bruce in 1323. The same family remained owners of Drum for the following 653 years. Irvine memorabilia is shown in the Family Room and the house contains an excellent collection of portraits and good Georgian furniture. It is a welcoming house with the feeling of a family home, enhanced by the recent creation of the Day and Night Nurseries.

The grounds contain the Old Wood of Drum – an ancient oak woodland with Site of Special Scientific Interest designation – mixed woodlands, three waymarked walks and an arboretum. Within the old walled garden is a fine collection of historic roses.

The property was bequeathed to the Trust in 1976 by Mr H Q Forbes Irvine of Drum along with an endowment.

A Castle, garden and grounds, Band B; garden and grounds only, Band E: see back flap

L Explanatory text in French, Dutch, German, Italian, Japanese, Spanish, Swedish

& Tearoom, shop, Pond Garden and Garden of Historic Roses. Access to ground floor of castle with assistance (one step). Toilet. Wheelchair available. Parking at castle and rose garden

Braille information sheets

Dog walks

(18) Open as castle

→ Off A93, 3m W of Peterculter, 10m W of Aberdeen and 8m E of Banchory. Bus: from Aberdeen Bus Station; tel Stagecoach Bluebird, (01224) 212266

OPEN	1 Apr to 31 May and 1 to 30 Sep, daily 12.30-5.30; 1 Jun to 31 Aug, daily 10-5.30.	Grounds, all year, daily 9.30-sunset.

Drum Castle, Garden & Estate

<Fyvie Castle>

FYVIE CASTLE

Fyvie, Turriff, Aberdeenshire, AB53 8JS. Tel (01651) 891266; fax (01651) 891107. Ranger service: tel (01330) 844651.

Fyvie was once a royal stronghold, one of a chain of fortresses throughout medieval Scotland. From 1390, following the Battle of Otterburn, five successive families created probably the finest example of Scottish Baronial architecture. An old tradition claims that these families – Preston, Meldrum, Seton, Gordon and Leith – each built one of Fyvie's five towers. An air of mystery is created by the ghosts and legends associated with this castle. The oldest part dates from the 13th century, and within its ancient walls is a great wheel-stair, the finest in Scotland. Contemporary panelling and plaster ceilings survive in the 17th-century Morning Room and the opulence of the Edwardian era is reflected in the interiors created by the first Lord Leith of Fyvie. A rich portrait collection includes works by Batoni, Raeburn, Romney, Gainsborough, Opie and Hoppner, and there is a fine collection of arms and armour, and 17th-century tapestries.

The grounds and loch were designed as landscaped parkland in the early 19th century. The 18th-century walled garden, has been redeveloped as a celebration of Scottish fruits and vegetables. Visitors can also enjoy the restored racquets court, ice house, bird hide, restored earth closet and beautiful lochside walks.

The castle, standing in 48 ha (118 a), was acquired by the Trust in 1984.

OPEN	1 Apr to 30 Jun and 1 to 30 Sep, Fri-Tue 12-5; 1 Jul to 31 Aug, daily 11-5.	Grounds, all year, daily, 9.30-sunset.

visit www.nts.org.uk

Fyvie Loch

<Haddo House

HADDO HOUSE

Ellon, Aberdeenshire, AB41 7EQ.
Tel (01651) 851440; fax (01651) 851888; email haddo@nts.org.uk

Unusual for Aberdeenshire in that it is not a castle, Haddo House is proud to be the most homely of the north-east of Scotland's great houses open to the public. Designed by William Adam for the 2nd Earl of Aberdeen in 1732, but refurbished in the 1880s, the House elegantly blends crisp Georgian architecture with sumptuous late Victorian interiors by Wright and Mansfield. Noted for its fine furniture, paintings and objets d'art, Haddo also boasts a delightful terrace garden with geometric rosebeds and fountain, commemorative trees, a lavish herbaceous border and secluded glades and knolls. A magnificent avenue of lime trees leads to Haddo Country Park with its lakes, monuments, walks and wildlife.

Throughout the house and grounds, personal portraits, monuments, plaques and memorabilia build up a fascinating account of the Gordon family who have lived at Haddo continuously for over 400 years. Paintings include works by Pompeo Batoni, William Mosman, Sir Thomas Lawrence and James Giles. Ecumenical chapel services most Sunday evenings in summer.

Haddo House, with its gardens, hall and stable block along with 73 ha (180 a) of the policies, was acquired by the Secretary of State for Scotland in 1978, through National Land Fund procedures, at the wish of the 4th Marquess of Aberdeen and Temair who also provided an endowment. The house and garden were opened by the Trust in July 1979. The adjacent Country Park, run by Aberdeenshire Council, was opened at the same time.

OPEN	**ALL ADMISSIONS (including members) FROM STABLES SHOP.** House, 1 to 30 Jun, Fri-Mon 11-4.30; 1 Jul to 31 Aug, daily 11-4.30. Guided tours only, departing at set times.	Shop and tearoom, Good Friday to Easter Monday, daily 11-5; 1 May to 30 Jun and 1 Sep to 31 Oct, Fri-Mon 11-5; 1 Jul to 31 Aug, daily 11-5.	Garden open all year, daily, 9.30-6.
	Aberdeenshire Council Country Park, open all year, daily 9.30-sunset.		

A Band B: see back flap

L Explanatory text in Dutch, French, German, Italian, Spanish

♿ House (lift for wheelchairs), garden and Country Park. Shop, restaurant, toilets. Wheelchairs available. Parking at Stable Block; disabled visitors may alight at house

🐕 Dog exercise area in Country Park

👜

🍵 (46) 'Taste of Scotland'. In historic Stable Block

🏃 ✳ 📖 **F P E** ☀

➡ Off B999, 4m N of Pitmedden, 19m N of Aberdeen and 10m NW of Ellon. 1m from National Cycle Route 1. Bus: from Aberdeen Bus Station; tel Stagecoach Bluebird, (01224) 212266

Key to Symbols
Please refer to the inside back flap of this guide for the key to symbols and price band information. Open out for easy reference.

Haddo House

Leith Hall, Garden & Estate>

A Band B; garden and grounds only, Band E: see back flap

L Explanatory text in Dutch, French, German, Italian and Spanish

& Ground floor of house; tearoom; pond walk.. Toilet. Wheelchair available. Parking at house

🍴 (28) 🎪 🏃 📖 **R**
P **E** ✳
→ On B9002, 1m W of Kennethmont and 34m NW of Aberdeen

LEITH HALL, GARDEN & ESTATE
Huntly, Aberdeenshire, AB54 4NQ. Tel (01464) 831216; fax (01464) 831594; email leithhall@nts.org.uk
Ranger service: tel (01330) 844651.

Leith Hall is a charming and intimate Scottish family home. It includes an interesting variety of family furniture, artwork, tapestry and military memorabilia. Exhibition – *For Crown and Country: the Military Lairds of Leith Hall*. The house offers visitors a unique insight into the lives, loves and tragedies of the Leith-Hay family over the last four centuries.

The 2.4-ha (6-a) garden features extensive herbaceous borders and a fine collection of alpines and primulas in the rock garden. At the top of the garden is a Chinese moon gate from where you can see spectacular views of the surrounding hills. Nearby is a small collection of Pictish stones. There are three waymarked walks through mixed woodland (the pond walk is suitable for pushchairs). Unique 18th-century stables, ice house.

Given by The Hon Mrs Leith-Hay in 1945.

OPEN	House and tearoom, Good Friday to Easter Monday, daily 12-5; 1 May to 30 Sep, Fri-Tue 12-5.	Garden and grounds, all year, daily 9.30-sunset.

For public transport information
Tel Traveline Scotland (0870) 6082608

visit www.nts.org.uk

Leith Hall

<Mar Lodge Estate

MAR LODGE ESTATE

Estate Office, Mar Lodge, Braemar, Aberdeenshire AB35 5YJ.
Tel (013397) 41433; fax (013397) 41432;
email marlodgeestate@nts.org.uk

The 29,380-ha (72,598-a) estate is part of the core area of the Cairngorms, internationally recognised as the most important nature conservation landscape in the British Isles. The estate contains four of the five highest mountains in the UK. It includes the upper watershed of the River Dee and remnant Caledonian pine forest of national importance. Some 7,080 ha (17,500 a) lie within the Cairngorms National Nature Reserve. Large parts of the estate are designated as Sites of Special Scientific Interest and the majority of it is within National Scenic Areas. The outstanding wildlife and birdlife on this prime example of a Highland estate are characteristic of the northern mountainous areas of Britain. Conservation work here includes reducing the red deer population to allow regeneration of the native Caledonian pine forest. Other ongoing work includes restoration of bulldozed tracks to footpaths, footpath repair and removal of deer fencing. The Trust is also actively conserving significant archaeology on the estate. There is pedestrian access to all the estate, including short- and long-distance walks. A range of guided walks on offer: contact Ranger Service.

Acquired in June 1995.

OPEN	Estate, all year, daily. Special 'open days' in 2003 for Lodge and Ballroom: 21 Apr (Easter Mon), Sun 6 Jul, Sun 7 Sep, 10-4. For 2004 dates, please contact property.

Ranger Service:
tel (013397) 41669.

Lodge caretaker:
tel (013397) 41427;
fax (013397) 41922.

♿ Area immediately surrounding Lodge. Access difficult in wider estate. Tours for groups of disabled visitors: tel Ranger Service for details

F
R
P At Linn of Dee
✷

➔ 5m W of Braemar. Access from A93 via an unclassified road. Bus: Aberdeen Braemar; tel Stagecoach Bluebird, (01224) 212266

Mar Lodge

Pitmedden Garden>

A Band C: see back flap

L Explanatory text in French, German, Italian, Spanish

Upper garden, museum, Visitor Centre, Nature Hut, tearoom. Toilet. Wheelchairs available

Dogs welcome on woodland trails

🛍 🐕 (28) 🎪 🔔 🚶 📖
R **P** ☀ ✳

→ On A920, 1m W of Pitmedden village and 14m N of Aberdeen. 2m from National Cycle Route 1. Bus: infrequent service passes road end; tel Stagecoach Bluebird, (01224) 212266

PITMEDDEN GARDEN

Ellon, Aberdeenshire, AB41 7PD. Tel (01651) 842352; fax (01651) 843188. Ranger service: tel (01330) 844651.

The centrepiece of this property is the Great Garden, originally laid out in 1675 by Sir Alexander Seton, 1st Baronet of Pitmedden. In the 1950s the elaborate floral designs were re-created under the guidance of the late Dr James Richardson; three of the formal parterres were taken from designs possibly used in the gardens at the Palace of Holyroodhouse, Edinburgh in 1647. The fourth parterre is a heraldic design based on Sir Alexander's coat-of-arms.

On the 40-ha (100-a) estate is the Museum of Farming Life, Visitor Centre, herb garden, ponds and woodland walk. New Nature Hut with interpretation of the wider estate.

The property was given to the Trust in 1952 with an endowment by Major James Keith. In 1978 the trustees of William Cook of Little Meldrum, Tarves, gave to the Trust a collection of agricultural and domestic artifacts, now part of the Museum of Farming Life, together with a pecuniary legacy.

OPEN	Garden, shop and tearoom, 1 May to 30 Sep, daily 10-5.30.	Grounds, all year, daily.

<Pitmedden Garden

The National Trust for Scotland

LOCHABER

Glencoe & Dalness

Set amid the brooding magnificence of Glencoe, the Trust's eco-friendly Visitor Centre has an exciting new interactive exhibition. The combination of vivid history and spectacular Highland scenery make this one of the most rewarding areas of Scotland for the visitor to explore.

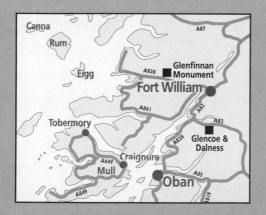

For more information contact
The National Trust for Scotland
HIGHLANDS &
ISLANDS REGION
Balnain House, 40 Huntly Street
Inverness IV3 5HR
Tel (01463) 232034

visit www.nts.org.uk

<Glencoe & Dalness

GLENCOE & DALNESS

The National Trust for Scotland Visitor Centre,
Glencoe, Argyll PH49 4LA.
Tel (01855) 811307, or (01855) 811729;
fax (01855) 812010; email glencoe@nts.org.uk

NEW

GLENCOE Visitor Centre

Green Tourism GOLD

A Band D: see back flap

L Explanatory text in Dutch, French, German, Italian, Japanese, Spanish

All Visitor Centre. Toilets. Parking at Centre

Large print interpretation; tactile displays

Induction loops

Details p 99

F

R **P** **E**

A82, 17m S of Fort William. Bus: services from Edinburgh, Glasgow and Fort William pass the Visitor Centre; tel Citylink, (0870) 505050

Some of the finest climbing and walking country in the Highlands is to be found within the 5,680 ha (14,035 a) in the Trust's care, in an area of dramatic landscapes and historical fact and legend. The infamous massacre of 1692 took place at many sites throughout the glen, but one of the main locations is just a short walk from the Trust's new eco-friendly Visitor Centre at Inverrigan.

Geologically, the Glencoe hills are significant as an example of a volcano collapsing in on itself during a series of violent eruptions. This is also an area of international botanical importance, particularly for the woodlands and Arctic alpine flora. In the lower part of Glen Coe the Trust owns a flock of sheep and fold of Highland cattle, part of a unique project to manage an area of internationally important grassland. The property includes a large Special Area of Conservation.

The A82 Glasgow to Fort William road runs through this spectacular glen and the Visitor Centre is a perfect stopping place for the traveller going north or south. Enjoy *Living on the Edge*, an interactive exhibition exploring the landscape, wildlife and history of this special place. Find out what it feels like to climb on ice; discover how the glen was formed; and try your hand at solving the conservation problems faced by the Trust.

5,180 ha (12,800 a) were purchased in 1935 and 1937. In 1972 the Trust purchased from the Forestry Commission the farm of Achnacon, in order further to safeguard amenity. In 1976 a Visitor Centre, built by the Countryside Commission for Scotland and run by the Trust, was opened at Clachaig. An Torr Woodland (1993) and Inverigan Campsite (1996) were purchased from Forest Enterprise.

OPEN	Site, all year, daily.	Visitor Centre, shop and café, 1 to 31 Mar, daily 10-4; 1 Apr to 31 Aug, daily 9.30-5.30; 1 Sep to 31 Oct, daily 10-5; 1 Nov to 28/29 Feb, Fri-Mon 10-4.

Key to Symbols
Please refer to the inside back flap of this guide for the key to symbols and price band information. Open out for easy reference.

visit www.nts.org.uk

Glenfinnan Monument

Bonnie Prince Charlie — Glenfinnan Monument

Glenfinnan Games take place on Saturday, 16 August, 2003 and Saturday 21 August, 2004.

A Band F: see back flap

L Audio programme in Dutch, French, Gaelic, German, Spanish

 Toilet. Exhibition, snack-bar and shop accessible. Wheelchair available. Parking at Centre

Induction loop

'Taste of Scotland'.

P Band I: see back flap

 A830, 18½m W of Fort William. Rail: Glenfinnan station 1m; tel (08457) 484950.

GLENFINNAN MONUMENT

NTS Information Centre, Glenfinnan, Highland, PH37 4LT.
Tel/fax (01397) 722250; email glenfinnan@nts.org.uk

Glenfinnan Monument, set amid superb Highland scenery at the head of Loch Shiel, was erected in 1815 by Alexander Macdonald of Glenaladale in tribute to the clansmen who fought and died in the cause of Prince Charles Edward Stuart. It was designed by the eminent Scottish architect James Gillespie Graham. The raising of the Prince's Standard took place at the head of the loch on 19 August, 1745, in the last attempt to reinstate the exiled Stuarts on the throne of Great Britain and Ireland. Despite its inspired beginnings and subsequent successes, the Prince's campaign came to its grim conclusion in 1746 on the battlefield at Culloden (see separate entry), also in the care of the Trust.

In the Visitor Centre are displays and an audio programme about the Prince's campaign from Glenfinnan to Derby and back to the final defeat at Culloden.

Handed over to the care of the Trust in 1938 by Sir Walter Blount, proprietor, on behalf of himself, the trustees of Glenaladale Estates and the Roman Catholic Diocese of Argyll and the Isles. A conservation agreement protecting 11 ha (27 a) surrounding the monument was made by Mr A MacKellaig.

OPEN	Site, all year, daily.	Visitor Centre, shop and snack-bar, 1 Apr to 30 Jun and 1 Sep to 31 Oct, daily 10-5; 1 Jul to 31 Aug, daily 9.30-5.30.

Glenfinnan Monument

The National Trust
for Scotland

WEST COAST ISLANDS

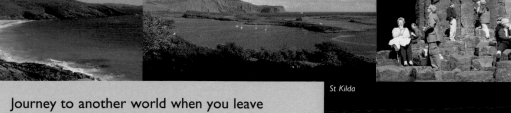

St Kilda

Journey to another world when you leave
the mainland behind to reach these, some of
the remotest properties owned by the Trust.
Whether it is the more accessible, yet
fascinating, sites on the Isle of Mull, or the
far-flung archipelago of St Kilda, a trip to
any of these islands is truly unforgettable.

For more information contact
The National Trust for Scotland
HIGHLANDS &
ISLANDS REGION
Balnain House, 40 Huntly Street
Inverness IV3 5HR
Tel (01463) 232034

visit www.nts.org.uk

Canna

Burg

Enquiries to Highlands and
Islands Regional Office; tel
(01463) 232034.

♿ Access extremely difficult

🐕 Dogs must be kept on a lead
at all times and cannot
negotiate the ladder
to the beach

📷📖 🔥

➡️ By footpath, 7m W of
Tiroran, off B8035 on N
shore of Loch Scridain.
Visitors' cars are not
permitted beyond the car
park at Tiroran. The fossil
tree is accessed via a
7-mile walk on a path which
becomes very rough and
precipitous and culminates in
a steep descent to the beach
by an iron ladder. The tree is
only accessible at low tide by
following the path.

♿ Access possible but difficult
by ferry

📷📖 🔥 ✳️

➡️ Ferry (no cars) from Mallaig,
Highland; tel Caledonian
MacBrayne, (01475) 650100.
Cruises from Mallaig and
Arisaig (see p 92)

Key to Symbols
Please refer to the inside
back flap of this guide for
the key to symbols and price
band information. Open out
for easy reference.

BURG
Isle of Mull, Argyll & Bute.

The exposed location of Burg, open to the full force of the Atlantic
weather, together with its colloquial name, 'The Wilderness', give an
indication of the wild terrain of this property. Volcanic eruptions many
millions of years ago formed the distinctive stepped outline of the
peninsula, as the molten lava cooled to form the cliffs which can be seen
today. Although the area is now almost devoid of trees, the sea cliff
beyond Burg Farm retains the impression of a tree, known as
MacCulloch's Fossil Tree, engulfed by the lava flow perhaps
50 million years ago.

The property lies within a National Scenic Area and includes a Special
Area of Conservation. The Trust has been working to conserve
important populations of plants and insects, including the rare slender
Scotch burnet moth.

The 569 ha (1,405 a) of this property were bequeathed to the Trust by Mr A Campbell Blair of Dolgelly in 1932.

OPEN	All year, daily.

CANNA
Inner Hebrides. Tel (01687) 462466.

The most westerly of the Small Isles, Canna is 5 miles long and
1¼ miles wide. Its cultural background, archaeology and ornithology
make it one of the most interesting islands in the Hebrides. Sustainable
farming and crofting systems are carried out on the island, which is a
Special Protection Area for its large population of seabirds, especially
shags, which nest in the cliffs of its dramatic shoreline. Canna is also a
Special Area of Conservation. Pony trekking is available.

*Canna, together with the adjacent island of Sanday, was transferred into the Trust's care in May 1981 at the wish
of the owner, Dr John Lorne Campbell, who also included his Celtic and Scottish library. The Trust, together with the
Hebridean Trust, have renovated St Edward's Church to provide a study centre for visitors.*

OPEN	All year, daily.

Iona>

Macquarie Mausoleum

IONA
SW of Mull, Argyll and Bute.

Iona is a small, fertile, crofting island, currently inhabited by around 130 people. The island is farmed largely by traditional methods. The Trust works in partnership with its tenant farmers to ensure that rare species, such as the corncrake, are conserved. For many centuries it has been an island of special significance for all Christians. In AD 563 Columba and his followers arrived here from Ireland to spread the gospel in Scotland and the north of England.

In the Trust's care, since December 1979, are 911 ha (2,250 a) of the island. The Abbey, other sacred buildings and historic sites were conveyed by the 8th Duke of Argyll in 1899 to the Iona Cathedral Trustees and are not owned by the Trust.

OPEN	All year, daily.

Enquiries to Highlands and Islands Regional Office; tel (01463) 232034.

A Payable at Abbey (not NTS: managed by Historic Scotland), including to Trust members

&. Access difficult but possible on ferry, to island roads and Abbey. No adapted toilets

(Not NTS)

(Not NTS)

(Not NTS)

➡ Ferry (no cars) from Fionnphort, Isle of Mull (A849). Ferry to Mull (Craignure) from Oban; tel Caledonian MacBrayne, (01475) 650100. Day excursions in summer, see p 92.

MACQUARIE MAUSOLEUM
Gruline, Isle of Mull, Argyll & Bute.

The Mausoleum is not Trust property but the Trust has, since 1963, managed it on behalf of the National Trust of Australia (New South Wales). Lachlan Macquarie, who was born nearby at Ulva Ferry in 1761, died in 1824 after distinguished service as Governor of New South Wales and was known as 'the father of Australia'. The Mausoleum is on the Gruline estate, which he owned.

OPEN	All year, daily.

Enquiries to Highlands and Islands Regional Office, tel (01463) 232034.

➡ Off B8035

visit www.nts.org.uk

For public transport information
Tel Traveline Scotland (0870) 6082608

<Mingulay, Berneray & Pabbay>

Enquiries to Highlands and
Islands Regional Office, tel
(01463) 232034.

📖📗 (not NTS)

MINGULAY, BERNERAY & PABBAY
Western Isles.

Until the last of the population left in 1912, crofting, fishing and fowling were central to the lives of the inhabitants of this island group.
As on St Kilda, the islanders used the seabirds and eggs for food and traded the feathers.

Mingulay (12 miles south of Barra) and Berneray together were made a Site of Special Scientific Interest in 1983 for the maritime vegetation, rock shore and cliff habitats found there, as well as for the seabird population. In 1994 the islands were made a Special Protection Area in recognition of the internationally important populations of breeding species of seabirds, particularly razorbill, guillemot, fulmar, kittiwake and shag. Storm petrel, common and Arctic terns, great skua, black guillemot, puffin and four species of gull also breed on the islands. The birds are attracted not only by the cliffs, coastal rocks and caves for nesting sites, but also by the fish supply in the area.

All the islands have significant archaeological sites, with several designated Scheduled Ancient Monuments, including the village area on Mingulay. The most northerly of the three islands, Pabbay, is separated from the smaller island of Rosinish by a tidal channel.

There are no facilities or services of any kind on the islands. All the islands have very high and dangerous cliffs and landing is difficult. The Barrahead lighthouse on Berneray, designed by Robert Stevenson and built in 1833, is not owned by the Trust. The Trust's management objectives for the islands, addressing such issues as seabirds, archaeology and vegetation management (grazing), are in the early stages of consideration.

Acquired in 2000 through a bequest by Miss Jean M Fawcett to provide an area of natural beauty in memory of her parents, Norman and Ethel, and the courage of her late brother, Bernard.

OPEN	All year, daily.

Key to Symbols
Please refer to the inside
back flap of this guide for
the key to symbols and price
band information. Open out
for easy reference.

visit www.nts.org.uk

ST KILDA NATIONAL NATURE RESERVE

Scotland's
National Nature
Reserves

Western Isles. Website: www.kilda.org.uk

Remote and spectacular, the St Kilda archipelago lies 41 miles west of Benbecula. It is the largest sea-bird colony in the north-east Atlantic, home to almost a million birds, including a quarter of the world's population of gannets. Its main island of Hirta maintained its population until 1930, when the islanders were evacuated at their own request. Fowling among the great colonies of seabirds (puffins for feathers and meat, young fulmars for oil and young gannets for meat) was the main employment, augmented by sheep herding, crofting and fishing. In addition to its NNR status (1957), St Kilda has been designated a Biosphere Reserve (1976), a scheduled Ancient Monument (1979), a National Scenic Area (1981), a Site of Special Scientific Interest (1984), Scotland's first World Heritage Site (1986) and a Special Area of Conservation (1992).

In 2003 the Trust, in conjunction with the Scottish Executive and other partners, is putting forward a nomination for the extension of St Kilda's World Heritage Site status to include the marine environment and cultural landscape. Bequeathed in 1957 by the 5th Marquess of Bute.

OPEN	All year, daily.

STAFFA NATIONAL NATURE RESERVE

Scotland's
National Nature
Reserves

W of Mull, Argyll & Bute.

This uninhabited island, only half-a-mile long by quarter-of-a-mile wide, is famous for its basaltic formations, distinctive stepped columns created when the lava of volcanic eruptions cooled many millions of years ago. These columns form the cathedral-like stature of Fingal's Cave, immortalised by Mendelssohn in his celebrated *Hebrides* overture. Other famous visitors to the island have included Queen Victoria and Prince Albert, the artist J M W Turner, and poets and writers Keats, Wordsworth, Tennyson and Sir Walter Scott. The island has important seabird populations, including a colony of puffins.

The island was given to the Trust in 1986 by John Elliott, Jr, of New York, as an imaginative way to honour the birthday of his wife Elly. She has been declared Steward of Staffa for her lifetime by the Trust. Donations to the necessarily high cost of improvements to landing facilities may be sent to Trust head office or placed in the donation box near the landing point on the island.

OPEN	All year, daily.

Enquiries to Highlands and Islands Regional Office; tel (01463) 232034.

♿ Access difficult but possible by boat

📖 (not NTS)

Each year, Trust work parties conserve and repair buildings, as well as carrying out archaeological work. Details on the work parties are available from NTS: see above. Information about visiting St Kilda on a Trust cruise is available from the Holidays Department at head office.

Enquiries to Highlands and Islands Regional Office; tel (01463) 232034.

♿ Access extremely difficult

➡ 7m W of Mull and 6m NE of Iona. Cruises from Iona, Mull and Oban. See p 92. Landing dependent on suitable weather conditions

The National Trust
for Scotland

ROSS-SHIRE

Inverewe Garden

Blessed by the warm currents of the North Atlantic Drift, the gems of this lovely and historic landscape are the surprisingly lush gardens at Lochalsh and Inverewe. Visitors to Inverewe in 2003 can join in the special celebrations to mark 50 years of Trust ownership.

**For more information contact
The National Trust for Scotland
HIGHLANDS &
ISLANDS REGION**
Balnain House, 40 Huntly Street
Inverness IV3 5HR
Tel (01463) 232034

visit www.nts.org.uk

Balmacara Square>

Lochalsh Woodland Garden

BALMACARA ESTATE & LOCHALSH WOODLAND GARDEN

Lochalsh House (NTS), Balmacara, Kyle, Ross-shire, IV40 8DN.
Tel (01599) 566325; fax (01599) 566359; email balmacara@nts.org.uk
Ranger/naturalist: tel (01599) 511231; fax (01599) 511417.

A crofting estate of 2,750 ha (6,795 a) with outstanding views of Skye and Applecross, and including the village of Plockton, an Outstanding Conservation Area. The estate also includes the Coille Mhór oakwood Special Area of Conservation (SAC). The neighbouring Loch Alsh is part of the Loch Alsh & Loch Duish marine SAC. Visitors can discover more about this secluded, fascinating area at the small Visitor Centre at Balmacara Square, where an interactive CD-ROM, guides to the extensive footpath network and other local information are available. The Visitor Centre is located within the recently restored farm steadings beside the old millpond. There are also craft workshops and a small delicatessen within the Square complex, an excellent spot for a picnic. Lochalsh Woodland Garden offers quiet sheltered walks by the lochside among mature Scots pine, oaks and beeches with developing collections of rhododendrons, fuchsias, bamboos, hydrangeas and ferns. Interpretation provided at the reception kiosk in the garden.

The Balmacara Estate was bequeathed to the Trust in 1946 by the late Lady Hamilton. Lochalsh House and policies were conveyed to the Trust by National Land Fund procedures in 1954. In 1999, the Trust completed the restoration and rehabilitation of Balmacara Square.

OPEN	Estate, all year.	Woodland garden all year, daily 9-sunset. Reception kiosk, 1 Apr to 30 Sep, daily 9-5. Balmacara Square Visitor Centre, 1 Apr to 30 Sep, daily 9-5 (Fri 9-4).

A Garden, Band F (CAC); Balmacara Square interpretation, Band G: see back flap

L Visitor Centre touchscreen programme in French, Gaelic, German, Italian and Spanish

& Visitor Centre in Square, lower reaches of garden (with care). Parking in Square and at Lochalsh House in garden

P At the Square and various other locations throughout the estate

→ A87, 3m E of Kyle of Lochalsh. Rail: stations at Kyle of Lochalsh, Plockton and Duirinish; tel (08457) 484950

Balmacara Estate

Lochalsh Woodland Garden

Corrieshalloch Gorge   Falls of Glomach

A Band F: see back flap

♿ Access difficult

☀

➡ A835 at Braemore,
12m SSE of Ullapool

CORRIESHALLOCH GORGE NATIONAL NATURE RESERVE

Braemore, Ross-shire.

Scotland's
National Nature
Reserves

This spectacular mile-long gorge, 61 m (200 ft) deep, is one of the finest examples in Britain of a box canyon. The river which carved this channel through hard metamorphic rock plunges 46 m (150 ft) over the Falls of Measach. The suspension bridge a little way downstream from the falls was built by John Fowler (1817-98), joint designer of the Forth Railway Bridge. Further downstream, a viewing platform provides an excellent vantage point looking up towards the falls.

Given in 1945 by John J Calder of Ardargie, 14 ha (35 a). A further 13 ha (32 a) were acquired from the Forestry Commission in 1994.

OPEN	All year, daily.

Also see Kintail.

📖 From Morvich Countryside Centre, Kintail

R

➡ NE of A87, 18m E of Kyle of Lochalsh

FALLS OF GLOMACH

Ross-shire. Ranger Service: tel (01599) 511231.

One of the highest waterfalls in Britain, 113 m (370 ft), set in a steep narrow cleft in remote country. The best approach is from the Morvich Countryside Centre (see Kintail), where Rangers may be available to give information. Or, for the very fit only, leave car by the Ling bridge, N end Loch Long, for a long walk along Glen Elchaig before making a steep climb to the Falls (7 miles – allow 8 hours). Ranger guided walks in summer.

890 ha (2,200 a) given by Mrs E G M Douglas of Killilan and Capt the Hon Gerald Portman of Inverinate in 1941.

OPEN	All year, daily.

For public transport information
**Tel Traveline Scotland
(0870) 6082608**

Falls of Glomach

Inverewe Garden>

50TH ANNIVERSARY EVENTS

INVEREWE GARDEN

Poolewe, Ross-shire, IV22 2LG.
Tel (01445) 781200; fax (01445) 781497; email inverewe@nts.org.uk

The sheer audacity of Osgood Mackenzie's vision in creating this outstanding 20-ha (50-a) garden, impressively set on a peninsula on the shore of Loch Ewe, is still astonishing today. The warm currents of the North Atlantic Drift or Gulf Stream help nurture an oasis of colour and fertility, where exotic plants from many countries flourish on a latitude more northerly than Moscow's. Himalayan rhododendrons, Tasmanian eucalypts, a large collection of New Zealand plants (including the National Collection of *Olearia*), diverse Chilean and South African introductions combine to give a colourful display throughout the year. Marked footpaths. Visitor Centre. Access to the wider estate.

The garden was created by Osgood Hanbury Mackenzie from 1863 and his work was carried on by his daughter Mairi T Sawyer who gave the 890-ha (2,000-a) Inverewe estate to the Trust in 1953 with an endowment for its upkeep.

OPEN	Garden, 1 Apr to 31 Oct, daily 9.30am-9pm (or sunset if earlier); 1 Nov to 31 Mar, daily 9.30-4. Visitor Centre and shop, 1 Apr to 30 Sep, daily 9.30-5; 1 to 31 Oct, daily 9.30-4. Restaurant, same dates, but opens at 10. Hours may be extended during 50th anniversary events in 2003: contact property for details.

A Band B: see back flap

L Guidebook in French and German; interpretation in French, German, Italian and Spanish.

& Some paths in garden, greenhouse, restaurant, shop, Visitor Centre. Toilets. Wheelchairs available. Parking at Visitor Centre

No dogs in garden, please. Limited shaded car parking

Camping Club campsite: details p 99

Well-stocked gift shop and plant centre

(180) 'Taste of Scotland'.

R Ranger-led estate walks May to Aug: booking advised

P ☀

➡ On A832, by Poolewe, 6m NE of Gairloch. Bus: Westerbus from Inverness; tel (01445) 712255

Inverewe Garden

Kintail & Morvich | Shieldaig Island | Strome Castle

A Band F: see back flap

♿ Countryside Centre. No toilet

➢ Morvich Caravan Site: details p 99

🚩📚 R

P At Countryside Centre

✳

➡ N of A87, 16m E of Kyle of Lochalsh

KINTAIL & MORVICH

Morvich Farm, Inverinate, Kyle, Ross-shire, IV40 8HQ.
Tel (01599) 511231; fax (01599) 511417.

A magnificent stretch of West Highland scenery, the 7,431-ha (18,362-a) estate includes the Falls of Glomach and the Five Sisters of Kintail – four of them over 915 m (3,000 ft). There is a Countryside Centre at Morvich Farm, off A87, which is also the best access point to the mountains and where Rangers may be available to give information. The site of the battle of Glen Shiel (1719) lies approximately 5 miles E of the village, beside the main road. Ranger-guided high-level walks in summer.

Purchased by the Trust in 1944.

OPEN	Estate, all year, daily.	Countryside Centre at Morvich (unstaffed), 1 Apr to 30 Sep, daily 9am-10pm.

For enquiries tel (01445) 791221; fax (01445) 791378.

➡ In Loch Torridon. Off Shieldaig, A896

SHIELDAIG ISLAND

Torridon, Ross-shire.

This 13-ha (32-a) island is almost entirely covered in Scots pine, which once formed vast forests covering much of the Scottish Highlands. The Trust acquired it in 1970.

OPEN	All year, daily.

For enquiries tel (01599) 566325, fax (01599) 566359.

➡ Off A896, 4½m SW of Lochcarron

STROME CASTLE

Ross-shire.

The ruined castle is romantically situated on a rocky promontory jutting into Loch Carron, commanding fine views westwards to Skye. First recorded in 1472 when it was a stronghold of the Lords of the Isles, it later belonged to the MacDonnells of Glengarry. Following a quarrel with Kenneth MacKenzie, Lord of Kintail, it fell in 1602 after a long siege and was blown up. All that remains of the tower is a heap of rubble but substantial sections of the wall of the adjacent hall still stand.

Presented in 1939 by Mr C W Murray of Couldoran.

OPEN	All year, daily.

Key to Symbols
Please refer to the inside back flap of this guide for the key to symbols and price band information. Open out for easy reference.

West Affric

<Torridon

TORRIDON

**Torridon Mains, Torridon, Achnasheen, Ross-shire, IV22 2EZ.
Tel (01445) 791221; fax (01445) 791378.**

A 6,500-ha (16,000-a) estate encompassing some of Scotland's finest mountain scenery, including Liathach, 1,054 m (3,456 ft), which has seven tops, and Beinn Alligin, 985 m (3,230 ft). The mountains, in addition to their scenic splendour, hold much of interest to geologists and naturalists. Liathach is of Torridonian sandstone some 750 million years old; the tops, of white quartzite some 150 million years younger. The estate includes part of the Beinn Eighe National Nature Reserve and a Special Area of Conservation.

A Trust Countryside Centre, with interpretive display, small shop and an audio-visual presentation on wildlife, is at the junction of A896 and the Diabaig road. There is also a Deer Museum located 600 yards on, down the road leading to The Mains. Herds of red deer and Highland cattle may be seen in the farm fields. There is a short walk along a shore path between Mol Mor, basic accommodation at the head of Loch Torridon, and the village.

The original estate of 5,706 ha (14,100 a) was accepted by the Commissioners of Inland Revenue in part satisfaction of estate duty ensuing upon the death of the 4th Earl of Lovelace; in May 1967 it was transferred to the care of the Trust through National Land Fund procedures. In 1968 the Trust was presented with a further 809 ha (2,000 a) at Wester Alligin, immediately to the west of the Torridon estate. The gift, in memory of Sir Charles Blair Blair Gordon, GBE, and Lady Gordon, was made by their sons, Blair, Howard and John.

OPEN	Countryside Centre, Good Friday to 30 Sep, daily 10-6.	Estate, Deer Enclosure and Deer Museum (unstaffed), all year, daily.

WEST AFFRIC

Ross-shire.

The Trust bought this important area in 1993 to protect its wild land character, to restore its natural flora and secure one of the most popular east/west paths in the Highlands, once part of the drove road from Skye to Dingwall. The 3,662 ha (9,050 a) join the Trust's Kintail and Glomach properties, making a total area of 11,100 ha (27,400 a) under Trust care. Basic accommodation is available at the Alltbeithe hostel (let to SYHA) and the Camban bothy (let to the Mountain Bothies Association).

OPEN	All year, daily.

A Band F: see back flap

& Ramp into Centre. Parking at Centre. Two steps into Deer Museum. Toilet 55 metres

R P

→ N of A896, 9m SW of Kinlochewe. Bus: Duncan MacLennan, tel (01520) 755239, connects to Strathcarron rail station (20m), daily Jun-Sep, Mon/Wed/Fri Oct-May. Post Bus, tel (01463) 256273 or 256228, connects to Achnasheen rail station (20m), all year Mon-Sat except public holidays

For enquiries
tel (01599) 511231,
fax (01599) 511417.

R

P At Kintail or the Forest Enterprise car park near Affric Lodge (OS Map 25 Ref 200 235), reached from Cannich on the A831

INVERNESS, NAIRN, MORAY & THE BLACK ISLE

The National Trust for Scotland

Culloden

The fascinating history of Scotland has a stronger presence here than anywhere else in the nation. The drama of Culloden, with its far-reaching effects on Scottish society, is vividly told by costumed actors on the battlefield. At Brodie, home of a noble family that has lived here since the 12th century, discover the wonderful art collection.

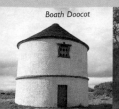
Boath Doocot

<Brodie Castle

BOATH DOOCOT
Auldearn, Nairn.

A 17th-century doocot on the site of an ancient motte. Montrose defeated the Covenanters nearby on 9 May 1645; a battle-plan is on display.

Presented by the late Brigadier J Muirhead of Boath, MC, in 1947.

OPEN	All year, daily.

A Band G: see back flap

Access difficult

Off A96, 2m E of Nairn, 1m from National Cycle Route 1

BRODIE CASTLE
Brodie, Forres, Moray IV36 2TE. Tel (01309) 641371; fax (01309) 641600; email brodiecastle@nts.org.uk

Brodie Castle is a fine 16th-century Z-plan tower house with 17th- and 19th-century additions, set in peaceful parkland. The family association with the area predates the castle, going back at least to Malcolm, Thane of Brodie, who died in 1285, and possibly to 1160, when it is believed Malcolm IV endowed the Brodies with their lands. The castle was damaged in an attack in 1645 by Montrose's army, but survived. It contains fine French furniture, English, Continental and Chinese porcelain, and a major collection of paintings, including 17th-century Dutch art, 19th-century English watercolours, Scottish Colourists and early 20th-century works. The magnificent library contains some 6,000 volumes.

The grounds are famous for their unique daffodil collection in spring. Explore them along the woodland walks, one by the edge of a 1.6-ha (4-a) pond with access to wildlife observation hides.

Brodie Castle, with its contents and 71 ha (175 a) of policies, was acquired by the Secretary of State for Scotland using National Land Fund procedures, at the wish of the present Brodie of Brodie, 25th Chief of that name, and transferred into the care of the Trust in 1980. Brodie of Brodie also provided an endowment.

OPEN	1 to 30 Apr and 1 Jul to 31 Aug, daily 12-4; 1 May to 30 Jun and 1 to 30 Sep, Sun-Thu 12-4.	Grounds, all year, daily 9.30-sunset.

A Band C; Garden, grounds and car parking, Band I: see back flap

L Explanatory text in Dutch, French, German, Italian, Japanese, Spanish, Swedish

Ground floor accessible with assistance (four steps). Toilets. Nature trail and hides. Wheelchair available by prior arrangement. Parking at castle

Audio-tape tour. Braille guide

Camping ground (youth organisations only)

(32) 'Taste of Scotland'.

Off A96, 4¹/₂m W of Forres and 24m E of Inverness. On National Cycle Route 1. Bus: Stagecoach Bluebird; tel (01343) 544222

For public transport information
Tel Traveline Scotland (0870) 6082608

visit www.nts.org.uk

Living history at Culloden>

Culloden

A Band C: see back flap

L Guidebook in French and German. AV programme in French, Gaelic, German, Italian, Japanese

Visitor Centre, shop, restaurant. Motorised wheelchair available. Toilet. Parking at Visitor Centre

Braille guidebook; raised map

Induction loop; subtitled AV programme; special AV channel

Bookshop

(80) 'Taste of Scotland'.

FPE

S27 B9006, 5m E of Inverness. On National Cycle Routes 1 and 7. Bus: Rapson's Coaches (No 12) from PO, Queensgate, Inverness; tel (01463) 710555; Guide Friday tour bus from Inverness, May to Sep; tel (01463) 224000. Rail: Inverness station 6m; tel (08457) 484950

CULLODEN

Culloden Moor, Inverness, Highland IV2 5EU.
Tel (01463) 790607; fax (01463) 794294; email culloden@nts.org.uk

The evocative scene of the last major battle fought on mainland Britain. The final Jacobite uprising ended here on 16 April, 1746, when the army of Prince Charles Edward Stuart was crushed by the Government forces, led by the Duke of Cumberland. Turf and stone dykes that played a crucial part in the battle have been reconstructed on their original site, and a small flock of Hebridean sheep is grazing here as they did in 1746, as part of the Trust's long-term project to remove scrub and so restore the field to its state at the time of the battle.

Relive the drama of Culloden at Living History presentations (summer only) in the original Leanach Cottage, which survived the battle being fought around it, and has been restored. Also in the Trust's care are the Graves of the Clans, the Well of the Dead, the Memorial Cairn, the Cumberland Stone and the Field of the English. The Visitor Centre houses a permanent Jacobite exhibition, including an 18th-century sampler commemorating the battle and a historical display.

The Graves, Memorial Cairn and King's Stables were presented by Hector Forbes of Culloden who also, for a nominal sum, sold the field in which the Cumberland Stone stands. Alexander Munro of Leanach presented 0.5 ha (1.2 a) in 1937 and in 1959 his son Ian Munro added 0.6 ha (1.5 a) to this gift. In 1981 the Trust purchased 44 ha (108 a) from the Forestry Commission. The Field of the English was purchased in 1989, and a further 6.3 ha (15 a) of adjacent land was purchased in 1998.

OPEN	Site all year, daily.	Visitor Centre, restaurant and shop, 1 Feb to 31 Mar and 1 Nov to 31 Dec, daily 11-4 (closed 24/25/26 Dec); 1 Apr to 30 Jun and 1 Sep to 31 Oct, daily 9-6; 1 Jul to 31 Aug, daily 9-7. Last audio-visual show half-an-hour before closing.

Culloden

<Hugh Miller's Cottage>

HUGH MILLER'S COTTAGE

Church Street, Cromarty, Ross-shire, IV11 8XA. Tel (01381) 600245.

Here in this thatched cottage built c1698 by his great-grandfather was born Hugh Miller, on 10 October, 1802. Miller rose to international acclaim as a geologist, editor and writer. The furnished cottage contains an exhibition and video on his life and work. To the rear is a Scottish 'wild garden' of colourful native plants, redesigned to reflect Miller's own love of nature. A reading room has been opened, offering visitors the chance to browse at leisure among Miller's works. New artworks on display include a tapestry, sculpture and silver medallion.

The cottage was first opened to the public in 1890. It was handed over to the Trust by Cromarty Town Council in 1938.

OPEN	Good Friday to 30 Sep, daily 12-5; 1 to 31 Oct, Sun-Wed 12-5.

A Band E: see back flap

L Explanatory text in French, Gaelic, German, Italian, Spanish

♿ Part of lower floor accessible. Steep steps to garden. Parking at cottage

Braille information sheets

P Public parking at shore

→ Via Kessock Bridge and A832, in Cromarty, 22m NE of Inverness. On National Cycle Route 1. Bus: Rapson's Coaches from Inverness; tel (01463) 710555

Culloden

The National Trust
for Scotland

NORTHERN ISLANDS

Fair Isle

Remote and wild, these beautiful outposts of
the Trust's portfolio reward the adventurous
traveller with unparalleled opportunities for
bird-watching and for witnessing the skill of
traditional crafts unknown elsewhere.

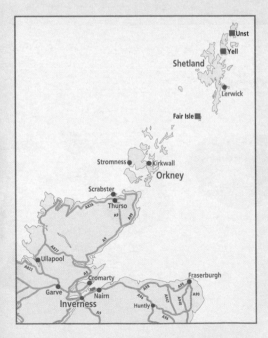

For more information contact
The National Trust for Scotland
HIGHLANDS &
ISLANDS REGION
Balnain House, 40 Huntly Street
Inverness IV3 5HR
Tel (01463) 232034

visit www.nts.org.uk

<Fair Isle

Unst & Yell

FAIR ISLE

Shetland, ZE2 9JU. Website: www.fairisle.org.uk

One of the most isolated inhabited islands in Britain. In a successful effort to stem depopulation, the Trust has encouraged and initiated various improvements, including a renewable energy project using wind power. The intricate, colourful knitted patterns, which take their name from the island, are famous and the Fair Isle Knitting Co-operative sells island knitwear world-wide. Additional crafts now include traditional wooden boat-building, spinning, weaving, dyeing, felting, locker-hooking, wood-turning and fiddle-making, and the manufacture of straw-backed chairs, spinning wheels and stained-glass windows.

Fair Isle is a bird-watcher's paradise. A warm welcome awaits visitors, with opportunities to observe exceptional flora, fauna, archaeology, spectacular cliff scenery and traditional crofting practices. The Trust, in partnership with the islanders and the Bird Observatory, is currently working on marine protection.

In 1948 Dr George Waterston, owner of the island, established the Fair Isle Bird Observatory Trust. In 1954, ownership passed to the Trust. The present observatory and lodge, built in 1969 with assistance from NTS, provides accommodation for 31 visitors.

OPEN	All year, daily.	Bird observatory open: 1 May to 31 Oct.

UNST & YELL

Shetland ZE2 9UT.

This estate, at the northern tip of Shetland and Britain, extends to 1,550 ha (3,830 a). It comprises ten parcels of land, eight of which are on Unst, and includes a number of houses and agricultural buildings. The smallest parcel is the 12-ha (30-a) island of Daaey, off Fetlar. Most of the land is in agricultural use and there is a first-class Shetland pony stud. Scenically the three west coast areas of Woodwick, Collaster and Lund are outstanding, with undulating hills, low rocky coastline, beaches, cliffs and voes, all typical of Unst as a whole. The area is of geological, archaeological, botanical and ornithological importance. There is an interesting wood – the only one on Unst – at Halligarth, containing mostly sycamores.

The estate has been gifted to the NTS but leased back to the donor, Joy Sandison, for her lifetime. Several members of Miss Sandison's family were prominent in the community, including Arthur Edmonston, a surgeon, his brother Laurence, a distinguished naturalist, and nephew Thomas, a botanist. His brother-in-law Henry Saxby wrote The Birds of Shetland, published in 1894, eleven years after his death.

OPEN	All year, daily.

Enquiries to Highlands & Islands Regional Office, tel (01463) 232034.

→ Regular summer sailings of mail boat, *Good Shepherd IV*, from Grutness, Shetland; tel Jimmy Stout, (01595) 760222; for flight details tel Loganair, (01595) 840246 (details p 92)

Fair Isle Lodge & Bird Observatory, Fair Isle, Shetland ZE2 9JU tel/fax (01595) 760258.

B&B accommodation is available at Schoolton Croft House, tel (01595) 760250 and Upper Leogh, (01595) 760248, and self-catering at Springfield Croft House, tel (01595) 760225.

Enquiries to Highlands & Islands Regional Office; tel (01463) 232034.

→ Ferry from Aberdeen to Lerwick, then (via two ferries) by hired car or bus to Unst: tel NorthLink ferries, (01856) 851144; Leask Coach & Car Hire Co (01595) 693162. For travel details tel Lerwick Tourist Information Centre, (01595) 840246, or Shetland Council Environment & Transport, (01595) 744872.

Dirleton Castle   Provost Ross's House   Threave Castle   Clava Cairns

ANTONINE WALL
Three sections along B816, W of Falkirk.
The Wall was built from the Forth to the Clyde about AD 142 and consisted of ditch, turf rampart and road, with forts every two miles. One of the Trust's sections includes Rough Castle, 3m W of Falkirk, the best preserved of the forts. Gifted by Kerse Estates, Mr C W Forbes of Callander in 1938.
Under the guardianship of Historic Scotland.
OPEN: All year

CASTLE CAMPBELL
Off A91, N of Dollar, Clackmannanshire.
Built in the late 15th century, this was once the home of the chief of Clan Campbell. John Knox is said to have preached here in the 16th century. Presented to the Trust in 1950 by Mr J E Kerr of Harvieston.
Under the guardianship of Historic Scotland.
OPEN: 1 Apr to 30 Sep, daily 9.30-6.30; 1 Oct to 31 Mar, Mon-Sat 9.30-4.30 (except Thu, pm and Fri, all day), Sun 2-4.30
A HS Band 1: see back flap. Free admittance to NTS members

CASTLEHILL
On A814, in Dumbarton.
1.6 ha (4 a) let to West Dunbartonshire Council. Given to the Trust in 1936 by Captain Angus Cunninghame Graham RN.
OPEN: All year

CLAVA CAIRNS
Off B9006, 5m E of Inverness, Highland.
Dating from around 2000 BC, these circular burial chambers are surrounded by standing stones. The cairns are among the most outstanding Scottish prehistoric monuments. Interpretation boards on site. Gifted by J G Murray of Culloden in 1945.
Under the guardianship of Historic Scotland.
OPEN: All year

CROOKSTON CASTLE
Brockburn Road, 4m SW of Glasgow city centre.
Early 15th-century tower house on the site of a 12th-century castle. Mary, Queen of Scots, and Darnley stayed here after their marriage in 1565. Gifted by Sir John Stirling Maxwell, Bt in 1931, it was the Trust's first property.
Under the guardianship of Historic Scotland.
OPEN: All year, daily 9.30-6. Key from cottage next door.

DIRLETON CASTLE
On A198, in Dirleton, East Lothian. Tel (01620) 850330.
Beautiful ruins dating back to 1225, with 14th/16th-century additions. The castle has had an eventful history, from its first siege by Edward I in 1298 until its destruction in 1650. The garden encloses a late 16th-century bowling green surrounded by yew trees. Sales kiosk and exhibition. Gifted in 1981 by Vice-Admiral B C E Brooke.
Under the guardianship of Historic Scotland.
OPEN: 1 Apr to 30 Sep, daily 9.30-6.30; 1 Oct to 31 Mar, Mon-Sat 9.30-4.30, Sun 2-4.30
A HS Band 1 (including to Trust members): see back flap

visit www.nts.org.uk

GLENLUCE ABBEY GLEBE
1½m NW of Glenluce, Dumfries & Galloway. Tel (01581) 300541.
Part of the glebe adjoining Glenluce Abbey, a ruined Cistercian abbey founded by Rolland, Lord of Galloway, in 1192. Purchased by the Trust in 1933.
Under the guardianship of Historic Scotland.
OPEN: 1 Apr to 30 Sep, daily 9.30-6.30; 1 Oct to 30 Nov, Mon-Sat 9.30-4.30 (except Thu, pm and Fri, all day), Sun 2-4.30; 1 Dec to 31 Mar, Sat 9.30-4.30, Sun 2-4.30
A (Abbey) HS Band 3 (including to Trust members): see back flap.

PARKLEA FARM
A8, off M8, 1m E of Port Glasgow, Inverclyde.
A strip of 27 ha (68 a) of land on the south bank of the Clyde, leased at a nominal rent to Inverclyde Council as a recreation ground. Bought from a bequest by Norman P Anderson in 1949.
OPEN: All year

PRESTON TOWER
Off A198, Prestonpans, East Lothian.
Adjacent to Hamilton House, Preston Tower was built by the Hamilton family in the 15th century; burned by Cromwell in 1650, then rebuilt with Renaissance addition on top. Also, 17th-century doocot and wall. Purchased by the Trust in 1969.
Under the guardianship of East Lothian Council.
OPEN: All year

PROVAN HALL
Auchinlea Road, Easterhouse, Glasgow G34 9QN. Tel (0141) 771 4399.
Built in the 15th century, this is probably the most perfect pre-Reformation mansion house in Scotland. Given to the Trust in 1938. Now part of Auchinlea Park, the property is managed by Glasgow City Council.
OPEN: All year, Mon-Fri 9-4.30 (except 25/26 Dec and 1/2 Jan and when special events are in progress)

PROVOST ROSS'S HOUSE (Aberdeen Maritime Museum)
Shiprow, Aberdeen AB1 2BY. Tel (01224) 337700.
Built in 1593, Provost Ross's House is the third oldest house in Aberdeen. In 1952, when in danger of demolition, the house was acquired from the Town Council, together with a substantial donation. It now houses part of the Aberdeen Maritime Museum, operated by the City of Aberdeen Council, which gives a wonderful insight into the rich maritime history of the city.
OPEN: All year, Mon-Sat 10-5, Sun 12-3

SCOTSTARVIT TOWER
Off A916, 2½m S of Cupar, Fife.
Situated three-quarters of a mile west of Hill of Tarvit Mansionhouse, this fine tower was known to have existed in 1579. Gifted, together with neighbouring Hill of Tarvit, by Miss E C Sharp in 1949.
Under the guardianship of Historic Scotland.
OPEN: as Hill of Tarvit Mansionhouse (see p24) (key at Mansionhouse).

THREAVE CASTLE
1m W of Castle Douglas, Dumfries & Galloway. Tel (07711) 223101.
This 14th-century Douglas stronghold stands on Threave Island in the River Dee. Gifted in 1948, together with neighbouring Threave House and garden, by Major A F Gordon DSO, MC.
Under the guardianship of Historic Scotland.
OPEN: 1 Apr to 30 Sep, daily 9.30-6.30; 1 Oct to 30 Nov, Mon-Sat 9.30-4.30 (except Thu, pm amd Fri, all day), Sun 2-4.30; 1 Dec to 31 Mar, closed.
A HS Band 2 (includes ferry) (including to Trust members): see back flap

ABERTARFF HOUSE
Church Street, Inverness, IV1 1EU.
Dating from the 16th century and one of the oldest houses in the burgh, Abertarff was presented to the Trust by the National Commercial Bank of Scotland in 1963. Its restoration, completed in 1966, was marked by a Civic Trust Award.

BALNAIN HOUSE
40 Huntly Street, Inverness IV3 5HR.
Built in 1726 as a merchant's house, Balnain was used as a field hospital for the Hanoverian troops during the battle of Culloden (1746). During the 1880s, it became the base of the Royal Ordnance for survey maps of the Highlands. After 17 years of restoration work by the Balnain House Trustees, it was opened in 1993 as 'the home of Highland music', but financial difficulties forced its closure in 2001. It now houses the Trust's Highlands and Islands Regional Office. Bought by the Trust in 1997.
Available for events and conferences: for further information tel (01463) 232034.

BEATON'S CROFT HOUSE
40 Bornesketaig, Kilmuir, Isle of Skye, IV51 9YS.
Acquired in 1997, Beaton's Croft House is a late 18th-century traditional Skye thatched house, situated in the crofting township of Bornesketaig at the north end of Skye.
The cottage is managed as self-catering accommodation: for bookings, tel Holidays Department at Trust head office. Special visits can occasionally be arranged: tel (01599) 566325.

CALANAIS BLACKHOUSE
Lewis, Western Isles.
Archaeological site of blackhouse, continuously altered and adapted from the mid-19th century up to the 1930s. Development under consideration. Acquired by the Trust in 1934.

HAMILTON HOUSE
Off A198, in Prestonpans, East Lothian.
Built in 1628 by John Hamilton, a prosperous Edinburgh burgess. Bought and restored by the Trust in 1937. House is let and open only by prior arrangement with NTS South Regional Office; tel (01721) 722502.

KIPPEN SMIDDY
Off A811, in Kippen, Stirling
Typical rural, early 18th-century blacksmith's shop forming part of a dwelling-house occupied by the same family of smiths from 1721 until 1986. Contains many authentic tools and artifacts. Gifted in 1982 by Andrew Rennie. May open to the public by prior arrangement: for information contact NTS West Regional Office, tel (0141) 616 2266.

LAMB'S HOUSE
Burgess Street, Edinburgh EH6 6RD.
This residence and warehouse of a prosperous merchant of the late 16th or early 17th century was renovated in the 18th century. The restoration of the exterior was completed in 1979 in association with Edinburgh and Leith Old People's Welfare Council. Presented in 1958 by Lord David Stuart, son of the 4th Marquess of Bute.

LINLITHGOW HOUSES
44-48 High Street, Linlithgow, West Lothian.
Two typical 16th- or 17th-century houses, restored in 1958 and let. Behind one is a rare late medieval oven. Given by Mr J G B Henderson in 1938.

NORTHGATE HOUSE
32 Northgate, Peebles, Borders.
A 'B'-listed stone house built around 1840, now converted into offices for the Trust's South Region. Purchased in 1996. Not open to view, but information available on Trust places to visit, events, membership, Thistle Camps and volunteer opportunities.

THE OLD GRANARY
West Mill Street, Perth.
Dating from the late 18th century, and restored by the Trust's Little Houses Improvement Scheme. Six flats for senior citizens were created on the upper floors. The ground floor is let to the Mountaineering Council of Scotland.

THE OLD SCHOOLHOUSE
Cottown, Perth & Kinross.
A unique, clay-built, thatched-roof cottage dating from the mid-18th century. Interpretive panel. Purchased by the Trust in 1993. Detailed technical advice is being provided by Historic Scotland. Future management and opening is under consideration. For information contact NTS North-East Regional Office; tel (01330) 833225.

PLEWLANDS HOUSE
South Queensferry, near Edinburgh.
Built in 1643, the house is of the L-plan design with the stair unusually placed half-way along the side of the north wing. Under the Trust's Little Houses Improvement Scheme, it has been restored to modern standards to provide private housing. Gifted by Irene Ferguson in 1953.

SAILOR'S WALK
Kirkcaldy, Fife.
17th-century group of merchants' houses restored in 1950, gaining a Civic Trust Award. Given in 1950 by Kirkcaldy Burgh Council.

STENHOUSE MANSION
Stenhouse Mill Lane, Edinburgh.
This was the home of Patrick Ellis, Edinburgh merchant, in the early 17th century; the date 1623 is above the doorway. Adapted by the Trust and let to the Secretary of State for the Environment as a conservation centre. Given by the Greyhound Racing Association in 1938.

MAKE THE MOST OF YOUR MEMBERSHIP–
JOIN YOUR LOCAL SUPPORT GROUP

The Trust has 37 support groups throughout Scotland (one in London) encouraging members to get together through a programme of social, cultural and fundraising events; also day outings, weekend trips and even holidays abroad. The groups provide vital help to the Trust in a variety of ways, helping with volunteer guiding, conservation work, membership recruitment and events at properties and in the wider community. They also raise some £120,000 annually for the Trust's work at national and local level. Details of events are published with *Scotland in Trust* magazine twice a year. Each group is independently run by a committee of honorary office bearers, with a liaison service at Head Office provided by Ann Johnstone and Richard Prentice, in the Development Department. If you would like more information on the activities or details on how to join, contact Ann or Richard on (0131) 243 9385/9340 and they will put you in contact with the appropriate group secretary.

- Aberdeen & District Members' Centre
- North-East Aberdeenshire Members' Centre
- West Aberdeenshire & Kincardine Members' Centre
- Angus Members' Centre
- Argyll Members' Group
- Ayrshire Members' Centre
- Banff & Moray Members' Centre
- Bearsden & Milngavie Members' Centre
- Borders Members' Group
- Dumfriesshire Members' Group
- Dundee Members' Group
- Eastwood & District Members' Centre

- Edinburgh Members' Centre
- East Fife Members' Centre
- West Fife Members' Centre
- Galloway Members' Group
- Glasgow Members' Centre
- Highland Members' Centre
- Inverclyde Members' Centre
- Lanarkshire Members' Group
- London Members' Centre
- East Lothian Members' Centre
- Motherwell District Members' Group
- Perth & Kinross Members' Group
- Stirling Members' Centre

- Friends of Alloa Tower
- Friends of Brodick Castle & Country Park
- Friends of Broughton House & Garden
- Friends of Greenbank Garden
- Friends of Malleny Garden
- Friends of Suntrap Garden
- Weaver's Cottage Support Group
- Companions of the David Livingstone Centre
- St Kilda Club
- Friends of The Georgian House
- Friends of Ben Lomond
- Friends of Crarae

Volunteers of the East Fife Members' Centre run a Trust shop at 146 South Street, St Andrews, Fife KY16 9EQ. Open 3 Feb to 31 Dec, Mon-Sat 10-4 (closed 11/12 Aug and 25/26 Dec).

visit www.nts.org.uk

Staffa

Mingulay

Canna

Excellent ferry services exist to carry visitors and their cars to a large number of Scottish islands. The major ferry company operating in the Hebrides and the Clyde is Caledonian MacBrayne. Smaller operators run daily, weekly or charter cruises to many of the smaller islands. Sailings to Staffa are operated from Iona, Ulva and Fionnphort, and there are inclusive day tours to Staffa, Iona and Mull from Oban. From Mallaig there is an improved service to the Small Isles – Rum, Eigg, Muck and Canna – which allows day trips to be made by passengers.

The Trust's two islands on Loch Lomond, Bucinch and Ceardach, can be viewed from some of the loch excursions operating from Balloch and Luss or the mail boat at Balmaha.

For details about opportunities to visit St Kilda by participating in a work party, contact the Trust's Highlands & Islands regional office, tel (01463) 232034. Fair Isle, lying between Orkney and Shetland, may be visited by *Good Shepherd IV*, sailing from Grutness, Shetland. Loganair flights from Tingwall, Shetland, may be available: check with the company.

Details about services may be obtained from Tourist Information Centres and the sources listed below.

MOST ISLANDS IN THE FIRTH OF CLYDE & WESTERN ISLES

Caledonian MacBrayne, Ferry Terminal, Gourock PA19 1QP. Tel: (01475) 650100; car reservations (0870) 5650000. Website: www.calmac.co.uk

CANNA, RUM, EIGG & MUCK

Caledonian MacBrayne. Tel: (01475) 650100 or (01687) 462403. Murdo Grant, Arisaig Harbour, Highland (by private charter). Tel: (01687) 450224; email info@arisaig.co.uk; website www.arisaig.co.uk.
Bruce Watt, Mallaig Harbour, Highland. Tel: (01687) 462233/462320; email brucewattmallaig@aol.com; website www.knoydart-ferry.co.uk

STAFFA & IONA

Caledonian MacBrayne, in conjunction with local operators, run day tours to Iona and Staffa from Oban in summer. Tel: (01475) 650100. Gordon Grant Marine Ltd, Achavaich, Isle of Iona. Tel: (01681) 700338; email fingal@staffatours.com; website www.staffatours.com. David B Kirkpatrick, Tigh-na-Traigh, Isle of Iona. Tel: (01681) 700358; email dk@staffatrips.f9.co.uk; website www.staffatrips.f9.co.uk. Iain Morrison ('Turus Mara'), Penmore Mill, Dervaig, Isle of Mull. Freephone (08000) 858786; email info@turusmara.com; website www.turusmara.com Bowman's Coaches (provide a link between the ferry terminals on Mull at Craignure and Fionnphort). Tel: (01631) 563221.

LOCH LOMOND

Sweeney's Cruises. Tel: (01389) 752376, fax (01389) 721082; email john.sweeney@talk21.com
Island Cruises; tel: (01436) 860257. MacFarlane's Mail Boat Cruises; tel: (01360) 870214; website www.balmahaboatyard.co.uk; email boatyard@macfarlaneandson.co.uk

FAIR ISLE

Good Shepherd IV. Tel:(01595) 760222. Loganair; tel: (01595) 840246 (charter flights from Shetland). British Airways (flights from mainland), tel (0845) 7733377.

ORKNEY & SHETLAND

NorthLink; tel (01856) 851144; website www.northlinkferries.co.uk. Loganair; tel (01595) 840246 (charter flights within Shetland); British Airways (0845) 7733377 (flights from mainland). Orkney Ferries; tel: (01856) 872044.

St Kilda

Iona

Iona

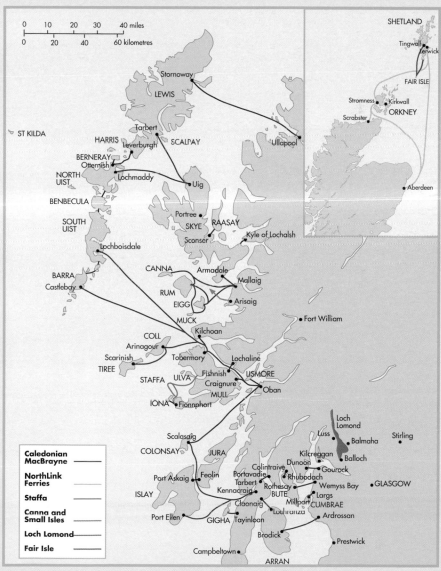

| 0 | 10 | 20 | 30 | 40 miles |
| 0 | 20 | 40 | 60 kilometres |

SHETLAND

Tingwall
Lerwick

FAIR ISLE

Stromness · Kirkwall
Scrabster · ORKNEY

· Aberdeen

Stornoway

LEWIS

Tarbert

HARRIS
Leverburgh
SCALPAY
BERNERAY
Otternish
NORTH
UIST
Lochmaddy
Uig

Ullapool

BENBECULA

SOUTH
UIST

Portree ·
SKYE RAASAY
Sconser · Kyle of Lochalsh

Lochboisdale

CANNA Armadale
Mallaig
RUM
EIGG Arisaig
MUCK

BARRA
Castlebay

Kilchoan
COLL
Arinagour
Scarinish Tobermory
TIREE Fishnish
STAFFA ULVA Lochaline
Craignure LISMORE
MULL
IONA Fionnphort Oban

· Fort William

Scalasaig
COLONSAY JURA

Loch
Lomond
Luss
Balmaha
Kilcreggan Balloch
Dunoon
Port Askaig Feolin Colintraive
Portavadie Gourock
Tarbert Rhubodach
ISLAY Kennacraig Rothesay Wemyss Bay
BUTE Largs
Claonaig Millport CUMBRAE
Port Ellen Lochranza Ardrossan
GIGHA Tayinloan
Brodick
Campbeltown · Prestwick
ARRAN

Stirling

· GLASGOW

ST KILDA

Caledonian
MacBrayne ———
NorthLink
Ferries ———
Staffa ———
Canna and
Small Isles ———
Loch Lomond ———
Fair Isle ———

Pitmedden Garden   Crarae Garden   Inverewe Garden   Threave Garden

Scotland is renowned internationally for the many fine gardens which flourish in its varied climate and which reflect its remarkable gardening heritage.

The National Trust for Scotland is the country's largest garden owner, with more than 283 hectares (700 acres) under intensive cultivation, supporting over 13,500 different sorts of plants. The Trust acquired its first garden in 1945 when it accepted Culzean Castle and seven years later added Brodick Castle, Falkland Palace and Pitmedden. Inverewe – the first property to be accepted primarily on its merit as an outstanding garden – was added in 1953. The developing portfolio now includes 35 major gardens and designed landscapes and about 30 smaller gardens.

Within this impressive selection, almost every style of Scottish garden history is represented – from the late-medieval at Culross Palace, through the 18th-century Picturesque (eg at Culzean), Victorian formality (eg at Haddo and House of Dun), early 20th-century plant-rich collections (eg Arduaine, Branklyn, Brodick, Crarae and Inverewe), to modern creations in older settings such as Falkland Palace, Inveresk Lodge and Priorwood.

Hand-in-hand with the maintenance of historic gardens, the Trust plays an important role in promoting the conservation of the art and craft of practical gardening – be it through maintaining the topiary hedges at Crathes Castle, or through the student training provided at its School of Practical Gardening at Threave.

Gardens are forever changing, usually as a result of the natural senescence of their plant components, but also because of pressures of public access and changes in fashion in garden design, plant availability and use. Conservation of gardens in Trust care must take account of these processes while ensuring that significant elements from their past are not lost.

If you would like to find out more about the gardens in Trust care, please contact the Gardens Department at head office.

SCOTLAND'S GARDENS SCHEME

Each year some 350 Scottish gardens, most of them privately owned, open their gates to the public under the banner of Scotland's Gardens Scheme. Founded in 1931, it is an independent charity and the money raised from garden visitors supports two main beneficiaries – the Queen's Nursing Institute (Scotland) and the Gardens Fund of The National Trust for Scotland.

The Scotland's Gardens Scheme handbook, available from selected Trust shops, or by post from the address below, lists the gardens open in each region month by month. These include Trust gardens, which nominate certain days when their entry money is donated to Scotland's Gardens Scheme.

On your travels round Scotland, keep an eye open for the distinctive yellow posters of the scheme advertising the local gardens that are open.

The Trust is particularly grateful to the garden owners and Scotland's Gardens Scheme for the magnificent financial support they provide each year to help maintain our own gardens.

Further information from Scotland's Gardens Scheme, 22 Rutland Square, Edinburgh EH1 2BB. Tel: (0131) 229 1870; fax: (0131) 229 0443; email: sgsoffice@aol.com

Puffin

Mar Lodge

West Affric

Red deer

The National Trust for Scotland cares for around 76,000 hectares (188,000 acres) of the most important and varied countryside. This includes a significant proportion of Scotland's coastline, from the dramatic islands of Fair Isle and St Kilda and the cliffs of St Abb's to the picturesque scenery of Culzean and Rockcliffe. Inland there are the wooded and farmed landscapes around many of the Trust's mansion houses. Perhaps most famous are the mountain properties – with one-sixth of all the Munros (mountains over 3,000 ft or 914 metres) on Trust properties. These are places for which Scotland is renowned and which attract visitors throughout the year.

The Trust's aims in looking after the countryside are to allow nature to thrive while enabling people to enjoy access. Every effort is also made to understand the imprint of previous generations, conserving the wealth of archaeological detail in the landscape. This often means trying to keep places as they are or managing change carefully, retaining the wild character that is so attractive. But 'preservation' usually requires active management. Ponds will naturally silt up with decaying vegetation; grasslands can become rank with tall grasses and even woodlands may be taken over by a few species, particularly if there has been a tradition of management in the past. Access too can become more difficult. Of course a balance must be struck between intervention and allowing natural processes. In wild areas in particular, and especially in the mountains, we do not seek to tame the wild but to respect it.

One outcome of nature and people living closely together, as they have in Scotland for over 5,000 years, is that some natural habitats, plant and animal species have been lost. The Trust is actively involved in ecological restoration – for example, using controlled grazing as a means of retaining many plants whose existence depends on light levels of grazing. In other places it is better to remove grazing to encourage woodlands and scrub to develop where it has been lost or diminished. The great pinewoods of the Cairngorms at Mar Lodge Estate are the subject of very intensive management, by reducing the level of grazing by deer. No one would deny that these forests have been managed in the past, often by planting and felling. Our approach today is to allow a more natural woodland environment to develop, together, we hope, with the wild birds and animals – red squirrel, wood ants, black grouse and capercaillie – that should live there.

This work depends on having the resources needed. In particular the Trust relies on the skills of its specialist conservation staff, including the rangers, and on volunteers. Practical work is underpinned by knowledge gained through survey and monitoring.

Scotland's Nature in Trust, **by writer and naturalist J Laughton Johnston, is an in-depth, lavishly illustrated study of the Trust's wildlife and crofting management on its countryside properties. It is published by A&C Black at £20.**

The Trust appointed its first ranger/naturalists back in 1970 and is now the largest ranger employer in Scotland, with 26 permanent and 25 seasonal staff, backed up by a number of long-term volunteers. A primary role of the service is to welcome visitors to our countryside estates and to help them enjoy their visit to the full. Each year, we lead over 500 guided walks and some 12,000 school pupils enjoy ranger-led activities.

Our rangers operate from 14 different services covering the Trust's varied and valued properties, from Inverewe to St Abb's Head, Mar Lodge Estate to Threave. They are in the front line in conserving archaeological features, wildlife habitats, rare plant and animal species and all of our treasured landscapes. Their work involves such diverse tasks as overseeing contracts to repair our upland paths; monitoring nesting seabirds; and protecting rare birds of prey. Rangers can be identified by the badge that is common to all services in Scotland (illustrated on this page). The Ranger Services in Dumfries & Galloway and the Lothians run volunteer groups.

To find out more about becoming a volunteer ranger, please call Fiona Chalmers on (01721) 726008.

The National Trust for Scotland gratefully acknowledges the continuing generous support of SNH towards its Ranger Service.

The Trust has developed a new and exciting initiative, Corporate Challenge, which is aimed at businesses and companies UK-wide and beyond. Using practical conservation work as a vehicle for staff development and team-building, Corporate Challenge offers companies the chance to take an active role in conserving important and fragile landscapes across Scotland, while developing their staff teams in a completely new and challenging environment.

Groups of up to 12 employees undertake a practical task which is not only a good teamwork experience but will have a lasting effect on the environment. In order to complete the practical task set, the group is encouraged to demonstrate various team skills including leadership, good communication, delegation and problem solving. The task presents employees, working in an environment away from the office, with an exciting, stimulating and fun challenge.

Based in beautiful and often remote countryside properties, the team stay in a Trust base camp and although food is provided, part of the team challenge is for the group to provide their own energy-fuelling 3-course evening meals. All work is supervised by Trust staff and extra-keen groups can undertake further intensive team-building exercises, programmed into the Challenge, if requested.

Corporate Challenge offers companies the opportunity to become directly involved in the conservation of Scotland's fragile landscapes. All proceeds made from Corporate Challenge will directly support further practical conservation work by contributing to the running costs of the Conservation Volunteer programme.

If you would like to find out more about Corporate Challenge, you can visit our website at: ntscorporatechallenge.org.uk or please call Julia on (0131) 243 9427 or email: jdownes@nts.org.uk

MAKE A DIFFERENCE

The National Trust for Scotland Conservation Volunteers carry out practical conservation work at countryside properties all over Scotland. Each year, up to 800 dedicated and enthusiastic volunteers work on 40 properties and complete up to 120 projects. Providing invaluable support to Trust property staff and ranger service, the volunteer workforce equates to approximately 16 full-time members of staff. Anyone over age 16, who would like the opportunity to help conserve Scotland's fragile landscapes and make a difference, is welcome. There are two ways to become involved: you can join one of the Conservation Volunteer local groups or take part on a Thistle Camp working holiday.

CONSERVATION VOLUNTEER LOCAL GROUPS

There are four local groups of conservation volunteers based in Glasgow, Edinburgh, Aberdeen and Perth/Dundee. Each group works on weekend or day projects throughout the year on countryside properties throughout Scotland. All projects are free and food, accommodation and transport are provided. No experience is necessary but you should be reasonably fit and enjoy working outdoors.

Benefits of joining one of the above groups include:
- free travel to new places, making new friends along the way
- working on the 'frontline', alongside our property staff
- learning new countryside skills and in doing so helping to conserve Scotland's countryside.

To request a copy of one of the local groups' seasonal work programmes email: conservationvolunteers@nts.org.uk or send an SAE to the NTS address below.

THISTLE CAMP WORKING HOLIDAYS

Thistle Camps are residential practical conservation projects, sponsored by TotalFinaElf Exploration UK plc, which last from between one and three weeks. The camps run between March and October each year and they take place in magnificent surroundings throughout Scotland. Popular locations include Grey Mare's Tail, Inverewe, Fair Isle and Crathes. The programme also includes the action-packed Trailblazers camps for 16-18-year olds, combining essential conservation work with adventure-type activities.

The work carried out on the camps is wide-ranging and interesting. Projects undertaken can include fencing, woodland management and the repair of the Trust's mountain footpaths. All work is supervised by a member of staff such as a ranger or gardener who can also provide background information to the area.

All you will need are old clothes, waterproofs, stout footwear and a warm sleeping bag. Accommodation is in a well-equipped Trust base camp or outdoor centre where volunteers help with the cooking and other domestic duties. Camps start at £50 (£35 unwaged) and prices vary depending on the time of year and the duration of the camp.

To find out more about our working holidays you can visit our website at: www.thistlecamps.org.uk. For a copy of the Thistle Camp brochure email: conservationvolunteers@nts.org.uk or send an SAE. to: Thistle Camps, NTS, Wemyss House, 28 Charlotte Square, Edinburgh EH2 4ET.

BASE CAMPS

Stay on or near our countryside properties at a price you and your family can afford. The Trust offers simple accommodation for groups at four of its properties, giving you the best early start to that energetic day on the hills.

SHORE LODGE, BRODICK
Situated within the grounds of Brodick Castle, Garden and Country Park on the Isle of Arran, this newly completed centre provides comfortable accommodation for up to 14. It is ideally situated for access to the shore, Goatfell and Brodick village. The Lodge has a sitting room with wood-burning stove, a fully equipped kitchen and a dining room. There is also a drying room, four WCs with wash-basins and three showers.

KINTAIL OUTDOOR CENTRE
This centre is situated 16 miles from Kyle of Lochalsh. It is on the banks of the River Croe, in an area of lochs and mountains offering a wide variety of outdoor pursuits. Countryside Rangers are on hand to help visiting groups make the most of their stay. The Centre has been completely refurbished and provides accommodation for up to 24 people. It comprises two wings sleeping ten, with WCs and showers, and a leaders' flat suitable for four. The Centre also has a fully equipped kitchen and dining room.

MAR LODGE ESTATE BASE CAMP
This new accommodation, part of the former Stable Block, is situated four miles west of Braemar, offering easy access to the Cairngorms. There are four bedrooms providing sleeping accommodation for 12 people. A kitchen, common room, dining room, WCs, showers, laundry and drying room are provided.

MOL MOR, TORRIDON
Mol Mor, part of a converted farm steading at the head of Loch Torridon, provides good quality accommodation for up to 10 people. The three rooms – two four-bedded and one two-bedded – are fitted with bunk beds. The kitchen is well equipped and there are laundry facilities, WCs and showers.

ST EDWARD'S CHURCH, CANNA
Standing proud on the small island of Sanday, next to Canna, St Edward's is one of the landmarks of the Hebrides. This deconsecrated church has been converted to provide quality accommodation for up to 12 people. One room sleeps four and four rooms sleep two, all in bunk beds. There is also a sitting room, dining room, study centre facilities including computers, laundry room, showers and kitchen. Central heating throughout.

For details of any of the above Base Camps, contact the Holidays Department, tel (0131) 243 9331, fax (0131) 243 9594, email holidays@nts.org.uk

CARAVANNING & CAMPING

CULZEAN CASTLE CAMPING AND CARAVANNING CLUB SITE
Tel (01655) 760627 (before 8pm). Situated in Culzean Country Park. Facilities include toilets (including disabled facility), chemical toilet emptying point, wash-basins, showers, laundry facilities, electrical hook-ups, payphone and children's play area. Non-members are welcome. Caravans, motor caravans, trailer tents and tents accepted. Open dates: March to October: 90 pitches.

INVEREWE GARDEN CAMPING AND CARAVANNING CLUB SITE
Tel (01445) 781249 (before 8pm). Site near shore of Loch Ewe and Poolewe village. Facilities include toilets (including disabled facility), chemical toilet emptying point, wash-basins, showers, laundry and dishwashing facilities, electrical hook-ups and availability of bottled gas. Non-members are welcome. Caravans, motor caravans, trailer tents and tents accepted. Open dates: May to October: 55 pitches.

MORVICH CARAVAN CLUB SITE
Inverinate, Lochalsh, Highland IV40 8HQ.
Tel (summer only): (01599) 511354. Site on banks of River Croe near Loch Duich.
Facilities include: toilets (including for the disabled), laundry and drying room, TV, gas and electric points, dishwashing, family games room, mother and baby room, hard standings. Waste points for motor caravans. Salmon and sea trout fishing available.
Open dates: April to October: 106 pitches (tent campers also accepted).

THE NATIONAL TRUST FOR SCOTLAND CARAVAN AND CAMPING SITE, GLENCOE
Glencoe, Highland PA39 4LA.
Tel: (01855) 811397 (summer) or (01855) 811278 (winter). Facilities include toilets (including disabled facilities), showers, chemical disposal point, cooking shelters, dishwashing facilities, electric hook-ups, payphone and shop.
Open dates: 1 April to 31 October: 150 pitches.

For information on accommodation in Trust cottages or castles, see page 48.

Trust properties offer limitless opportunities to all sectors of education. Primary, secondary, tertiary and community groups are all welcome and specific visits or activities may be arranged to match the requirements of visiting students and groups. Our network of regional education officers will be happy to advise you and help prepare for visits to Trust properties. School parties are always welcome and education staff are always available to talk to teachers, either individually or in groups, and offer advice. 5-14 curriculum work is particularly well catered for and our staff are keen to help with project- and topic-based learning; some properties have specialist education staff to help with visits.

Opportunities exist at our countryside properties for environmental education outdoors and we have our own extensive ranger service. Many of our smaller properties offer the opportunity to study the built environment. Our facilities include costumes, history-based drama activities, spaces for project work and study boxes with objects for handling, which may also be borrowed for use in schools. For Standard Grade, Higher Still and SVQ work, enquiries about property details such as architecture, decorative art, paintings, gardens and natural history are welcomed by our department. Students of tourism, ecology and environmental studies may also find our properties a useful resource. Many of our properties are excellent venues for drama and workshop-based activities.

www.ntseducation.org.uk

A range of educational publications – including property-based study packs, special children's guides and leaflets – complement a visit and facilitate further study. Every property has an educational leaflet detailing facilities and what is available. To encourage educational visits we are able to offer Educational Membership. This not only allows a teacher or lecturer a free preliminary tour before each visit, but thereafter it allows the school, college or group free visits to all properties throughout the year's membership. New schools' programme available on request.

The Trust is committed to a policy of lifelong learning. In addition to formal education programmes, a variety of informal education activities is available. Our educational website at www.ntseducation.org.uk has a wealth of information for teachers, students and pupils looking for help with projects. New multimedia CD titles on Alexander 'Greek' Thomson/Holmwood, The Georgian House/New Town and the St Abb's Head marine reserve are available.

In addition to providing specialist educational services, the Trust enhances the visitor experience through its interpretation. Interpretation can take a variety of forms from leaflets and information panels to audio-visual tours, multi-media exhibitions and living history displays.

For further information on facilities, services and membership please contact the Education Department at head office. Tel (0131) 243 9313, fax (0131) 243 9301, email education@nts.org.uk; website www.ntseducation.org.uk

Or contact your regional Trust office (see addresses page 6).

St Margaret's, Restalrig, before and (right) after restoration

St Francis Friary, Gorbals, Glasgow

In parallel to its work caring for over 100 properties held in its permanent portfolio, the Trust also promotes the built heritage through its Little Houses Improvement Scheme (LHIS). The Scheme began formally in 1960, although this type of conservation activity had been carried out since the very earliest days of the Trust in the 1930s. It aims to repair and revive historic buildings on a revolving fund basis – bringing derelict historic buildings back to life and securing their future by conversion to an economically sustainable use. Buildings are then sold on to a private owner, with a conservation agreement in place to ensure a level of protection for the building in the long term.

Many of the early LHIS projects addressed the very real threat to the characteristic vernacular buildings of the East Neuk of Fife. The attractiveness of the Fife fishing villages today is due in no small part to the efforts of the LHIS. As historic buildings have become increasingly popular as homes, priorities for the Scheme have changed. It is now the large and complex buildings that are more under threat than the 'Little Houses' of the Scheme's title. Conservation of such properties not only protects and promotes their heritage merit, but can also have a wider benefit, acting as a catalyst in regenerating the surrounding area.

LHIS staff are always interested to hear of any potential projects. For any further information, contact the LHIS office on (0131) 243 9446, or email lhis@nts.org.uk

SCOTLAND'S CHURCHES SCHEME

Scotland's Churches Scheme is fast becoming an established part of Scottish life. This is demonstrated by the number of churches included in its handbook, *Churches to Visit in Scotland*, available from major booksellers or from the address below. The current edition includes many additional entries, and draws the attention of a wide public to this remarkable architectural heritage. Many of Scotland's most important buildings are abbeys and churches – not just the great and expansive, but also the small and humble, which are often found in the most beautiful and tranquil of settings. They all represent the rich cultural background of Scotland and the diversity of the nation.

Further information from Scotland's Churches Scheme, Dunedin, Holehouse Road, Eaglesham, Glasgow G76 0JF. Tel: (01355) 302416; website: www.churchnet.ucsm.ac.uk/scotchurch

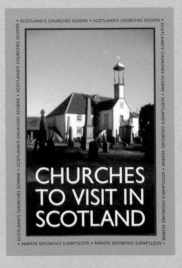

CHURCHES TO VISIT IN SCOTLAND

The National Trust
for Scotland

COASTLINES & ISLANDS
SEE THEM IN STYLE

The Trust has been running annual cruises since 1953, visiting interesting countries and their adjacent islands. On every journey, our team of renowned experts and lecturers enables passengers to understand and enjoy destinations to their utmost. The Trust charters the *Black Prince*, which carries 400 passengers and 200 crew and was refitted in late 2002/early 2003. The ship is renowned for its friendly atmosphere, especially on Trust cruises, due to their 'special interest' itineraries, which have proved over the years to be extremely popular.

We run two cruises a year: a one-week holiday around the Scottish coastline and islands and the traditional two-week cruise which goes further afield. We've been as far as Spitsbergen, St Petersburg, Oporto and Reykjavik, and all our cruises sail from and return to Scottish ports.

Call (0131) 243 9334 for current details, or visit the website on www.nts.org.uk, or email cruises@nts.org.uk

OPENING TIMES & ADMISSION CHARGES QUICK REFERENCE GUIDE - FOR FULL PROPERTY DETAILS SEE PAGES IN GUIDE

DUMFRIES & GALLOWAY

	pg	JAN	FEB	MAR	APR	MAY	JUN	JUL	AUG	SEP	OCT	NOV	DEC	ADMISSION CHARGES
BROUGHTON HOUSE	8					Mon-Sat 11-5, Sun 1-5								Adult £2, concession £1 (honesty box).
BROUGHTON HOUSE GARDEN	8		Mon-Fri 11-4			House may be closed during 2003 and for part of the 2004 season for major conservation works: please check with property.					as Feb			no charge
BRUCE'S STONE	8							open all year						no charge
THOMAS CARLYLE'S BIRTHPLACE	8						Thur-Mon 1-5							Adult £2.50, concession £1.90, adult group £2, child group/school group £1, family £7.
GREY MARE'S TAIL NATURE RESERVE	9							open all year						no charge
MURRAY ISLES	9							open all year						no charge
ROCKCLIFFE	9							open all year						no charge
THREAVE ESTATE & GARDEN	10					open all year, daily 9.30-sunset								House & Garden Adult £9, concession £6.50, adult group £7, child group/school group £1, family £23. Garden only Adult £5, concession £3.75, adult group £4, child group/school group £1, family £13.50.
THREAVE HOUSE							Wed, Thu, Fri and Sun, 11-4 (guided tours only, maximum 10 people, two per hour, admission by timed ticket).							
WALLED GARDEN & GLASSHOUSES						open all year, daily 9.30-5								
VISITOR CENTRE	10	daily 10-4					daily 9.30-5.30					daily 10-4		
VENNIEHILL	10							open all year						no charge

SCOTTISH BORDERS

	pg	JAN	FEB	MAR	APR	MAY	JUN	JUL	AUG	SEP	OCT	NOV	DEC	ADMISSION CHARGES
HARMONY GARDEN	12				open Easter*			Mon-Sat 10-5, Sun 1-5						Adult £2, concession £1 (honesty box).
PRIORWOOD GARDEN & DRIED FLOWER SHOP	12				open Easter*	Mon-Sat 12-5, Sun 1-5		Mon-Sat 10-5, Sun 1-5			Mon-Sat 12-5, Sun 1-5			Adult £2.50, concession £1.90, adult group £2, child group/school group £1, family £7.
TRUST SHOP				Mon-Sat 12-4				Mon-Sat 10-5, Sun 1-5						
ROBERT SMAIL'S PRINTING WORKS	13				open Easter*			Thu-Mon 12-5, Sun 1-5						Adult £3.50, concession £2.60, adult group £2.80, child group/school group £1, family £9.50.
ST ABB'S HEAD	13							open all year						£2 (Contribute and Conserve)
NATURE RESERVE CENTRE							daily 10-5 (groups by appointment)							

EDINBURGH (cont over)

	pg	JAN	FEB	MAR	APR	MAY	JUN	JUL	AUG	SEP	OCT	NOV	DEC	ADMISSION CHARGES
CAIY STANE	16							open all year						no charge
N° 28 CHARLOTTE SQUARE SHOP	16							Mon-Sat 10-5						no charge
DRAWING ROOM GALLERY								Mon-Fri 11-3						
COFFEE HOUSE & RESTAURANT								Mon-Sat 9.30-5						Restaurant reservations (0131) 243 9339
THE GEORGIAN HOUSE	17			daily 11-3				daily 10-5					daily 11-3	Adult £5, concession £3.75, adult group £4, child group/school group £1, family £13.50.
GLADSTONE'S LAND	17							Mon-Sat 10-5, Sun 2-5						Adult £3.50, concession £2.60, adult group £2.80, child group/school group £1, family £9.50.

*Easter 2003 - 18-21 April. Easter 2004 - 9-12 April. Opening times are correct at the time of going to print. We recommend that, if possible, you double-check with the property you intend to visit, before you set out.

OPENING TIMES & ADMISSION CHARGES QUICK REFERENCE GUIDE - FOR FULL PROPERTY DETAILS SEE PAGES IN GUIDE

& THE LOTHIANS

Property	pg	Opening times	ADMISSION CHARGES
HOUSE OF THE BINNS	18	daily except Friday 2-5 (Jun–Sep)	Adult £5, concession £3.75, adult group £4, child group/school group £1, family £13.50
HOUSE OF THE BINNS PARKLAND		daily 10-4 (Feb–Mar); daily 10-7 (Apr–Sep); daily 10-4 (Oct–Dec)	
INVERESK LODGE GARDEN	18	open all year, daily, 10-6 or dusk if earlier	Adult £2, concession £1 (honesty box)
MALLENY GARDEN	19	open all year, daily, 10-6 or dusk if earlier	Adult £2, concession £1 (honesty box)
NEWHAILES HOUSE	19	Thu-Mon 12-5 visit to house by guided tour only - booking advised; Sat/Sun 12-5 (Oct)	Adult £7, concession £5.25, adult group £5.60, child group/school group £1, family £19
NEWHAILES POLICIES		open all year, daily, 10-6	£2 (Contribute and Conserve)
PRESTON MILL	20	Thu-Mon 12-5, Sun 1-5	Adult £3.50, concession £2.60, adult group £2.80, child group/school group £1, family £9.50

FIFE

Property	pg	Opening times	ADMISSION CHARGES
BALMERINO ABBEY	22	open all year	Adult £2, concession £1 (honesty box).
CULROSS PALACE, STUDY, TOWN HOUSE	22	open Easter*; daily 12-5 (Jun–Aug); Shop open Sat/Sun 12-4 (Nov–Dec)	Adult £5, concession £3.75, adult group £4, family £13.50.
CULROSS PALACE GARDEN		open all year, daily 10-6 or sunset if earlier	
FALKLAND PALACE	23	shop open check with property (Feb); Mon-Sat 10-6 Sun 1-5 (Mar–Oct); shop open daily 10-4 (Nov–Dec)	Adult £7, concession £5.25, adult group £5.60, child group/school group £1, family £19.
FALKLAND PALACE GARDEN		open all year, daily 10-6 or sunset if earlier	Adult £3.50, concession £2.60, adult group £2.80, child group/school group £1, family £9.50.
HILL OF TARVIT MANSIONHOUSE	24	daily 1-5 (tearoom opens at 12); Sat/Sun 1-5 (Oct)	Adult £5, concession £3.75, adult group £4, child group/school group £1, family £13.50.
HILL OF TARVIT GARDEN		open all year, daily, 9.30-sunset	£2 (Contribute and Conserve).
KELLIE CASTLE	24	open Easter*; daily 1-5 (tearoom opens at 12) (Jun–Aug)	Adult £5, concession £3.75, adult group £4, child group/school group £1, family £13.50.
KELLIE CASTLE GARDEN		open all year, daily, 9.30-sunset	£2 (Contribute and Conserve).

AYRSHIRE & ARRAN

Property	pg	Opening times	ADMISSION CHARGES
BACHELORS' CLUB	26	Fri-Tue 1-5 (morning visits available for pre-booked groups)	Adult £2.50, concession £1.90, adult group £2, child group/school group £1, family £7.
BRODICK CASTLE	26	daily 11-4.30 (morning visits available for pre-booked groups); daily 11-3.30 (Oct)	Adult £7, concession £5.25, adult group £5.60, child group/school group £1, family £19.
RECEPTION CENTRE		daily 10-4.30 (shop & walled garden 10-4.30, restaurant 11-5); Fri, Sat, Sun 10-3.30 (Nov–Dec)	Adult £3.50, concession £2.60, adult group £2.80, child group/school group £1, family £9.50. Nov-Mar £1 (honesty box).
BRODICK COUNTRY PARK		open all year, daily	no charge
GOATFELL	27	open all year, daily	no charge
CULZEAN CASTLE	28	daily 10.30-5 (last entry 4)	Combined Castle & Park Adult £9, concession £6.50, adult group £7, child group/school group £1, family £23.
CULZEAN COUNTRY PARK		open all year, daily, 9.30-sunset	Adult £5, concession £3.75, adult group £4, child group/school group £1, family £13.50. Nov-Mar £2 (CAC)
CULZEAN CASTLE VISITOR CENTRE		daily 9-5.30; Sat/Sun 11-4 (Nov–Dec)	

* Easter 2003 - 18-21 April Easter 2004 - 9-12 April. Opening times are correct at the time of going to print. We recommend that, if possible, you double-check with the property you intend to visit, before you set out.
Contribute and Conserve is a small charge for parking and use of facilities, which goes towards the long-term conservation of the property.

OPENING TIMES & ADMISSION CHARGES QUICK REFERENCE GUIDE - FOR FULL PROPERTY DETAILS SEE PAGES IN GUIDE

Property	pg	Opening Times (JAN–DEC)	ADMISSION CHARGES
OTHER CULZEAN VISITOR FACILITIES	28	daily 10.30-5.30	
SOUTER JOHNNIE'S COTTAGE	29	Fri-Tue 11.30-5	Adult £2.50, concession £1.90, adult group £2, child group/school group £1, family £7.
GREATER GLASGOW & CLYDE VALLEY			
BLACK HILL	32	all year, daily	no charge
CAMERONIANS' REG. MEMORIAL	32	all year, daily	no charge
GREENBANK GARDEN	32	all year, daily, 9.30-sunset	Adult £3.50, concession £2.60, adult group £2.80, child group/school group £1, family £9.50.
GREENBANK HOUSE		every Sun 2-4	
GREENBANK SHOP & TEAROOM		daily 11-5 (Sat/Sun 2-4 Jan/Feb & Nov/Dec)	
HOLMWOOD HOUSE	33	daily 12-5 (morning visits available for pre-booked groups)	Adult £3.50, concession £2.60, adult group £2.80, child group/school group £1, family £9.50.
HUTCHESONS' HALL	33	Mon-Sat 10-5 (hall on view subject to functions in progress)	Adult £2, concession £1
KITTOCHSIDE	34	all year, daily, 10-5 (closed 25/26 Dec and 1/2 Jan)	Adult £3, concession £1.50
DAVID LIVINGSTONE CENTRE	35	Mon-Sat 10-5, Sun 12.30-5	Adult £3.50, concession £2.60, adult group £2.80, child group/school group £1, family £9.50.
POLLOK HOUSE	36	all year daily, 10-5 (closed 25/26 Dec and 1/2 Jan)	Adult £5, concession £3.75, adult group £4, child group/school group £1, family £13.50. (Nov-Mar free)
POLLOK COUNTRY PARK		gardens, country park and Burrell Collection all year, daily	
THE TENEMENT HOUSE	37	daily 1-5 (weekday morning visits available for pre-booked groups)	Adult £3.50, concession £2.60, adult group £2.80, child group/school group £1, family £9.50.
WEAVER'S COTTAGE	37	Fri-Tue 1-5 (morning visits available for pre-booked groups)	Adult £3.50, concession £2.60, adult group £2.80, child group/school group £1, family £9.50.
ARGYLL, BUTE & LOCH LOMOND			
ARDUAINE GARDEN	39	all year, daily, 9.30-sunset	Adult £3.50, concession £2.60, adult group £2.80, child group/school group £1, family £9.50.
ARDUAINE RECEPTION CENTRE	39	daily, 9.30-4.30	
BEN LOMOND	39	all year, daily	no charge
BUCINCH & CEARDACH	40	all year, daily	no charge
CRARAE GARDEN	40	all year, daily, 9.30-sunset	Adult £3.50, concession £2.60, adult group £2.80, child group/school group £1, family £9.50.
CRARAE GARDEN VISITOR CENTRE	40	daily 10-5	
GEILSTON GARDEN	41	daily 9.30-5 (house not open)	Adult £2.50, concession £1.90, adult group £2, child group/school group £1, family £7.
THE HILL HOUSE	42	daily 1.30-5.30 (groups should pre-book) (weekday morning visits available for pre-booked groups)	Adult £7, concession £5.25, family £19 (no group rates).
TIGHNABRUAICH VIEWPOINT	42	all year, daily	no charge

Easter 2003 - 18-21 April Easter 2004 - 9-12 April. Opening times are correct at the time of going to print. We recommend that, if possible, you double-check with the property you intend to visit, before you set out.

OPENING TIMES & ADMISSION CHARGES QUICK REFERENCE GUIDE - FOR FULL PROPERTY DETAILS SEE PAGES IN GUIDE

CENTRAL SCOTLAND

Property	pg	Opening Times	Admission Charges
ALLOA TOWER	44	daily 1-5 (weekday mornings visits available for pre-booked groups)	Adult £3.50, concession £2.60, adult group £2.80, child group/school group £1, family £9.50.
BANNOCKBURN	45	site all year, daily	
BANNOCKBURN HERITAGE CENTRE	45	daily 10.30-4; daily 10-5.30 (last audio-visual show half-an-hour before closing); daily 10.30-4	Adult £3.50, concession £2.60, adult group £2.80, child group/school group £1, family £9.50.
BEN LAWERS	45	site all year, daily	£1 (honesty box) £2 (Contribute and Conserve)
BEN LAWERS INFORMATION CENTRE		daily 10-5 (may close or half-an-hour between 1 and 2)	
CUNNINGHAME GRAHAM MEMORIAL	46	all year, daily	no charge
DOLLAR GLEN	46	all year, daily	no charge
MENSTRIE CASTLE	46	Easter Sun*; Wed and Sun 2-5	no charge
MOIRLANICH LONGHOUSE	47	Easter Sun*; Wed and Sun 2-5	Acult £2, concession £1 (honesty box).
THE PINEAPPLE	47	grounds, all year, daily 9.30-sunset	no charge

PERTHSHIRE

Property	pg	Opening Times	Admission Charges
BRANKLYN GARDEN	50	Fri-Tue 10-5; daily 10-5; Fri-Tue 10-5	Adult £5, concession £3.75, adult group £4, child group/school group £1, family £13.50.
CRAIGOWER	50	all year, daily	no charge
DUNKELD (ELL SHOP)	51	Mon-Sat 10-5.30, Sun 12.30-5.30; Mon-Sat 10-4.30, Sun 12.30-4.30	£2 (Contribute and Conserve)
THE HERMITAGE	51	all year, daily	£2 (Contribute and Conserve)
KILLIECRANKIE	52	site, all year, daily	£2 (Contribute and Conserve)
KILLIECRANKIE VISITOR CENTRE		daily 10-5.30; daily 9.30-5; daily 10-5.30	£2 (Contribute and Conserve)
LINN OF TUMMEL	52	all year, daily	no charge

ANGUS

Property	pg	Opening Times	Admission Charges
ANGUS FOLK MUSEUM	54	Fri-Tue 12-5; daily 12-5; Fri-Tue 12-5	Adult £5, concession £3.75, adult group £4, child group/school group £1, family £13.50.
J M BARRIE'S BIRTHPLACE	54	Fri-Tue 12-5; daily 12-5; Fri-Tue 12-5	Adult £5, concession £3.75, adult group £4, child group/school group £1, family £13.50 (combined with Camera Obscura).
BARRY WATER MILL	55	Fri-Tue 12-5	Adult £5, concession £3.75, adult group £4, child group/school group £1, family £13.50.
CAMERA OBSCURA	55	daily 12-5 (last viewing 4.40)	Adult £5, concession £3.75, adult group £4, child group/school group £1, family £13.50 (combined with J M Barrie's Birthplace).
FINAVON DOOCOT	56	all year, daily - keys from Finavon Hotel	no charge
HOUSE OF DUN	56	Fri-Tue 12-5; daily 12-5 (guided tours only); Fri-Tue 12-5	Adult £7, concession £5.25, adult group £5.60, child group/school group £1, family £19.
ESTATE & MONTROSE BASIN NATURE RESERVE		all year, daily, 9.30-sunset	£1 (honesty box).

* Easter 2003 - 18-21 April. Easter 2004 - 9-12 April. Opening times are correct at the time of going to print. We recommend that, if possible, you double-check with the property you intend to visit, before you set out. Contribute and Conserve is a small charge for parking and use of facilities, which goes towards the long-term conservation of the property.

OPENING TIMES & ADMISSION CHARGES QUICK REFERENCE GUIDE - FOR FULL PROPERTY DETAILS SEE PAGES IN GUIDE

ABERDEEN & GRAMPIAN

Property	pg	JAN	FEB	MAR	APR	MAY	JUN	JUL	AUG	SEP	OCT	NOV	DEC	ADMISSION CHARGES
CASTLE FRASER, GARDEN & ESTATE	58				Fri-Tue 12-5.30 →			daily 11-5.30 →		Fri-Tue 12-5.30				Adult £7, concession £5.25, adult group £5.60, child group/school group £1, family £19.
CRAIGIEVAR CASTLE	59				Fri-Tue 12-5.30 (guided tours only - no coaches, no groups) →					→				Adult £9, concession £6.50, adult group £7, child group/school group £1, family £23.
CRAIGIEVAR CASTLE GROUNDS		all year, daily, 9.30-sunset →												£1 (Contribute and Conserve)
CRATHES CASTLE & VISITOR CENTRE	60					daily 10-5.30 →					daily 10-4.30			Combined Ticket Adult £9, concession £6.50, adult group £7, child group/school group £1, family £23.
CRATHES CASTLE GARDEN & ESTATE		all year, daily, 9-sunset →												Castle/walled garden & grounds only Adult £7, concession £5.25, adult group £5.60, child group/school group £1, family £19.
CRATHES RESTAURANT & SHOP			Wed-Sun 10-4 →		daily 10-5.30 →						daily 10-4.30		Wed-Sun 10-4	£2 (Contribute and Conserve)
DRUM CASTLE	61				daily 12.30-5.30 →		daily 10-5.30 →			as April				Adult £7, concession £5.25, adult group £5.60, child group/school group £1, family £19.
DRUM CASTLE GARDEN & ESTATE		all year, daily, 9.30-sunset →												Adult £2.50, concession £1.90, adult group £2, child group/school group £1, family £7.
FYVIE CASTLE	62				Fri-Tue 12-5 →			daily 11-5 →		as April				Adult £7, concession £5.25, adult group £5.60, child group/school group £1, family £19.
FYVIE CASTLE GROUNDS		all year, daily, 9.30-sunset →												£2 (Contribute and Conserve)
HADDO HOUSE	63				open Easter*	Fri-Mon 11-4.30 (guided tours only) →		daily 11-4.30 →		Fri-Mon 11-5 →				Adult £7, concession £5.25, adult group £5.60, child group/school group £1, family £19.
HADDO HOUSE SHOP & TEAROOM					open Easter*	Fri-Mon 11-5 →		daily 11-5 →		Fri-Mon 11-5 →				
HADDO HOUSE GARDEN		all year, daily, 9.30-6 → (Aberdeenshire Council Country Park, open all year, daily, 9.30-sunset)												
LEITH HALL	64				Fri-Tue 12-5 →			daily 12-5 →		Fri-Tue 12-5				Adult £7, concession £5.25, adult group £5.60, child group/school group £1, family £19.
LEITH HALL GARDEN & ESTATE		all year, daily, 9.30-sunset →												Adult £2.50, concession £1.90, adult group £2, child group/school group £1, family £7.
MAR LODGE ESTATE	65	open days for Lodge & ballroom 21 Apr/Sun 6 Jul/Sun 7 Sep, 10-4. For 2004 dates contact property												no charge
PITMEDDEN GARDEN, SHOP & TEAROOM	66					daily 10-5.30 →								Adult £5, concession £3.75, adult group £4, child group/school group £1, family £13.50.
PITMEDDEN GROUNDS		all year, daily →												

LOCHABER

Property	pg	JAN	FEB	MAR	APR	MAY	JUN	JUL	AUG	SEP	OCT	NOV	DEC	ADMISSION CHARGES
GLENCOE & DALNESS		all year, daily →												
GLENCOE VISITOR CENTRE	69	Fri-Mon 10-4 →				daily 9.30-5.30 →				daily 10-5 →			Fri-Mon 10-4	Adult £3.50, concession £2.60, adult group £2.80, child group/school group £1, family £9.50.
GLENFINNAN MONUMENT	70		daily 10-4 →			all year, daily →								Glenfinnan Games Sat 16 Aug 2003/Sat 21 Aug 2004
GLENFINNAN VISITOR CENTRE					daily 10-5 →			daily 9.30-5.30 →		daily 10-5 →				Adult £2, concession £1 (honesty box).

* Easter 2003 - 18-21 April. Easter 2004 - 9-12 April. Opening times are correct at the time of going to print. We recommend that, if possible, you double-check with the property you intend to visit, before you set out. Contribute and Conserve is a small charge for parking and use of facilities, which goes towards the long-term conservation of the property.

OPENING TIMES & ADMISSION CHARGES QUICK REFERENCE GUIDE - FOR FULL PROPERTY DETAILS SEE PAGES IN GUIDE

WEST COAST ISLANDS

Property	pg	JAN–DEC	ADMISSION CHARGES
BURG	72	all year, daily	no charge
CANNA	72	all year, daily	no charge
IONA	73	all year, daily	Admission payable at Abbey, including Trust members
MACQUARIE MAUSOLEUM	73	all year, daily	no charge
MINGULAY, BERNERAY & PABBAY	74	all year, daily	no charge
ST KILDA	75	all year, daily	no charge
STAFFA	75	all year, daily	no charge

ROSS-SHIRE

Property	pg	Opening times	ADMISSION CHARGES
BALMACARA ESTATE	77	all year, daily	Adult £2, concession £1 (Contribute and Conserve).
LOCHALSH WOODLAND GARDEN		all year, daily; 9-sunset	
RECEPTION KIOSK		daily 9-5	£1 (honesty box)
BALMACARA SQUARE CENTRE	78	daily 9-5 (Fri 9-4)	
CORRIESHALLOCH GORGE	78	all year, daily	Adult £2, concession £1 (honesty box).
FALLS OF GLOMACH	78	all year, daily	no charge
INVEREWE GARDEN	79	daily 9.30-4 (Jan–Mar); daily 9.30am-9pm (or sunset if earlier); daily 9.30-4 (Dec)	Adult £7, concession £5.25, adult group £5.60, child group/school group £1, family £19. Hours may be extended during 50th Anniversary events in 2003: contact property for details
INVEREWE VISITOR CENTRE		daily 9.30-5 (restaurant opens at 10); daily 9.30-4 (Oct–Nov)	
KINTAIL & MORVICH ESTATE	80	all year, daily	Adult £2, concession £1 (honesty box).
MORVICH COUNTRYSIDE CENTRE	80	daily 9am-10pm	
SHIELDAIG ISLAND	80	all year, daily	no charge
STROME CASTLE	80	all year, daily	no charge
TORRIDON ESTATE	81	Estate, deer enclosure and deer museum (unstaffed) all year, daily	
TORRIDON COUNTRYSIDE CENTRE		daily 10-6	Adult £2, concession £1 (honesty box).
WEST AFFRIC	81	all year, daily	no charge

* Easter 2003 - 18-21 April Easter 2004 - 9-12 April. Opening times are correct at the time of going to print. We recommend that, if possible, you double-check with the property you intend to visit, before you set out. Contribute and Conserve is a small charge for parking and use of facilities, which goes towards the long-term conservation of the property.

OPENING TIMES & ADMISSION CHARGES QUICK REFERENCE GUIDE - FOR FULL PROPERTY DETAILS SEE PAGES IN GUIDE

	pg	JAN	FEB	MAR	APR	MAY	JUN	JUL	AUG	SEP	OCT	NOV	DEC	ADMISSION CHARGES
INVERNESS, NAIRN ...														
BOATH DOOCOT	83	all year, daily												£1 (honesty box).
BRODIE CASTLE	83				daily 12-4	Sun-Thu 12-4				Sun-Thu 12-4				Adult £5, concession £3.75, adult group £4; child group/school group £1, family £13.50.
BRODIE CASTLE ESTATE				all year, daily 9.30-sunset										£1 (Contribute and Conserve).
CULLODEN	84	all year, daily												Adult £5, concession £3.75, adult group £4; child group/school group £1, family £13.50.
CULLODEN VISITOR CENTRE	85		daily 11-4		daily 9-6		daily 9-7			daily 9-6		daily 11-4 (closed 24/25/26 Dec)		
HUGH MILLER'S COTTAGE						daily 12-5				Sun-Wed 12-5				Adult £2.50, concession £1.90 adult group £2; child group/school group £1, family £7.
N. ISLANDS														
FAIR ISLE	87	all year, daily												no charge
FAIR ISLE BIRD OBSERVATORY						daily								
UNST & YELL	87	all year, daily												no charge

* Easter 2003 - 18-21 April Easter 2004 - 9-12 April Opening times are correct at the time of going to print. We recommend that, if possible, you double-check with the property you intend to visit, before you set out.
Contribute and Conserve is a small charge for parking and use of facilities, which goes towards the long-term conservation of the property.

Alphabetical index of properties owned or managed by The National Trust for Scotland and open to the public

	page		page
Alloa Tower	44	Craigievar Castle	59
Angus Folk Museum	54	Craigower	50
Arduaine Garden	39	Crarae Garden	40
Bachelors' Club	26	Crathes Castle, Garden & Estate	60
Balmacara Estate & Lochalsh Woodland Garden	77	Culloden	84
Balmerino Abbey	22	Culross	22
Bannockburn	45	Culzean Castle & Country Park	28
J M Barrie's Birthplace	54	Cunninghame Graham Memorial	46
Barry Water Mill	55	Dollar Glen	46
Ben Lawers National Nature Reserve	45	Drum Castle, Garden & Estate	61
Ben Lomond	39	Dunkeld	51
Black Hill	32	Fair Isle	87
Boath Doocot	83	Falkland Palace, Garden & Old Burgh	23
Branklyn Garden	50	Falls of Glomach	78
Brodick Castle, Garden & Country Park	26	Finavon Doocot	56
Brodie Castle	83	Fyvie Castle	62
Broughton House & Garden	8	Geilston Garden	41
Bruce's Stone	8	The Georgian House	17
Bucinch & Ceardach	40	Gladstone's Land	17
Burg	72	Glencoe & Dalness	69
Caiy Stane	16	Glenfinnan Monument	70
Camera Obscura	55	Goatfell	27
Cameronians' Regimental Memorial	32	Greenbank Garden	32
Canna	72	Grey Mare's Tail Nature Reserve	9
Thomas Carlyle's Birthplace	8	Haddo House	63
Castle Fraser, Garden & Estate	58	Harmony Garden	12
Nº 28 Charlotte Square	16	The Hermitage	51
Corrieshalloch Gorge Nature Reserve	78	The Hill House	42

	page		page
Hill of Tarvit Mansionhouse & Garden	24	Priorwood Garden & Dried Flower Shop	12
Holmwood House	33	Rockcliffe	9
House of the Binns	18	St Abb's Head National Nature Reserve	13
House of Dun & Montrose Basin Nature Reserve	56	St Kilda National Nature Reserve	75
Hutchesons' Hall	33	Shieldaig Island	80
Inveresk Lodge Garden	18	Robert Smail's Printing Works	13
Inverewe Garden	79	Souter Johnnie's Cottage	29
Iona	73	Staffa National Nature Reserve	75
Kellie Castle & Garden	24	Strome Castle	80
Killiecrankie	52	The Tenement House	37
Kintail & Morvich	80	Threave	10
Kittochside, the Museum of Scottish Country Life	34	Tighnabruaich Viewpoint	42
Leith Hall, Garden & Estate	64	Torridon	81
Linn of Tummel	52	Unst & Yell	87
David Livingstone Centre	35	Venniehill	10
Macquarie Mausoleum	73	Weaver's Cottage	37
Malleny Garden	19	West Affric	81
Mar Lodge Estate	65		
Menstrie Castle	46		
Hugh Miller's Cottage	85		
Mingulay, Berneray & Pabbay	74		
Moirlanich Longhouse	47		
Murray Isles	9		
Newhailes	19		
The Pineapple	47		
Pitmedden Garden	66		
Pollok House	36		
Preston Mill & Phantassie Doocot	20		

Editor Hilary Horrocks
Design HGDesign

Photographs
Sue Anderson; Niall Benvie; Val Bissland; John Boak; Ian Boyter; J G Burgess;
Ben Buxton; Laurie Campbell; Brian Chapple; Kathy Collins; Val Corbett;
Douglas Corrance; Dennis Coutts; George A Dey; Lesley Doctor; Allan Forbes;
John Forgie; Alex Gillespie; Tony Gorzkowski; HG Design; Jim Henderson;
Martin Hind, Positive Image; Cameron Lees; Mark A Leman; Douglas MacGregor;
David N McIntyre; Cailean MacLean; George McLeod; Anthony MacMillan;
Lea MacNally; Frank McShane; David Mardon; Ian Mitchell; NTS Library;
Jim Nicholson; Ben Notley; Bill Robertson; David Robertson; Isla Robertson;
Tom Robertson; Joe Rock; Glyn Satterley; Mairi Semple; Sidney Shear;
Alasdair Smith; Jonathan Smith; Andy Thompson; Shannon Tofts;
Dave Wheeler; Whitehouse Studios; Harvey Wood

Origination CMR Origination
Print Pindar plc

Published by The National Trust for Scotland © 2003
Wemyss House, 28 Charlotte Square, Edinburgh EH2 4ET

ISBN 0 901625 77 9
2648 P 180m-1/03

All information in this Guide is correct at time of going to print.